D0205608

# The North Atlantic Treaty Organization

*The North Atlantic Treaty Organization* provides an incisive analysis of the Atlantic Alliance and clearly outlines all of NATO's key facets to deliver an authoritative account.

Detailing the origins, structure, workings and activities of this institution, the volume examines the past of the Alliance to put NATO's future in context as the institutional basis for the security dimension of the transatlantic relationship, and as an institution vital to global security.

The book is divided into three sections:

- Cold War NATO
- Strategic Vacation
- New Age NATO

Commencing with the impact of 11 September 2001 on the Alliance, the reader is taken through NATO's story to demonstrate the political robustness of an alliance continually in political crisis, from its foundation in 1949, as the threat posed by the Soviet Union waxed and waned, through to the difficulties caused by NATO's lack of political cohesion. Having established the timeline, the book provides a snapshot of NATO today, its members, structure and mission and the new tasks for which it must prepare. The book concludes by considering the challenges the Alliance must face as it prepares for the big security dilemmas of the twenty-first century, the differences in both strategy and power of Americans and Europeans, and the contrast between yesterday's NATO and today's.

*The North Atlantic Treaty Organization* is essential reading for all students of politics and international relations and will be of interest to all readers who wish to acquire an excellent understanding of this key force in world affairs.

**Julian Lindley-French** is currently a Senior Scholar at the Center for Applied Policy, Ludwig Maximilians University, Munich and Senior Associate Fellow of the Defence Academy of the United Kingdom. His recent works include *A European Defence Strategy* (Gütersloh: Bertelsmann Stiftung, 2004), *A Chronology of European Security and Defence 1945–2005* (Geneva: Geneva Centre for Security Policy, 2005) and *Why Europe Needs to Be Strong . . . and the World Needs a Strong Europe"* (Gütersloh: Bertelsmann Stiftung, 2005).

**Routledge Global Institutions**
Edited by Thomas G. Weiss
*(The CUNY Graduate Center, New York, USA)* and
Rorden Wilkinson
*(University of Manchester, UK)*

The "Global Institutions Series" is designed to provide readers with comprehensive, accessible, and informative guides to the history, structure, and activities of key international organizations. Every volume stands on its own as a thorough and insightful treatment of a particular topic, but the series as a whole contributes to a coherent and complementary portrait of the phenomenon of global institutions at the dawn of the millennium.

Books are written by recognized experts, conform to a similar structure, and cover a range of themes and debates common to the series. These areas of shared concern include the general purpose and rationale for organizations, developments over time, membership, structure, decision-making procedures, and key functions. Moreover, current debates are placed in historical perspective alongside informed analysis and critique. Each book also contains an annotated bibliography and guide to electronic information as well as any annexes appropriate to the subject matter at hand.

The volumes currently published or under contract include:

**The United Nations and Human Rights (2005)**
A Guide for a New Era
*by Julie A. Mertus (American University)*

**The UN Secretary-General and Secretariat (2005)**
*by Leon Gordenker (Princeton University)*

**United Nations Global Conferences (2005)**
*by Michael G. Schechter (Michigan State University)*

**The UN General Assembly (2005)**
*by M.J. Peterson (University of Massachusetts, Amherst)*

**The Commonwealth(s) and Global Governance**
*by Timothy Shaw (Royal Roads University)*

**The Organization for Security and Co-operation in Europe**
*by David J. Galbreath (University of Aberdeen)*

**UNHCR**
The Politics and Practice of Refugee Protection Into the Twenty First Century
*by Gil Loescher (University of Oxford), James Milner (University of Oxford), and Alexander Betts (University of Oxford)*

**The World Health Organization**
*by Kelley Lee (London School of Hygiene and Tropical Medicine)*

**The World Trade Organization**
*by Bernard Hoekman (World Bank) and Petros Mavroidis (Columbia University)*

**The International Organization for Standardization and the Global Economy**
Setting Standards
*by Craig Murphy (Wellesley College) and JoAnne Yates (Massachusetts Institute of Technology)*

**The International Olympic Committee**
*by Jean-Loup Chappelet (IDHEAP Swiss Graduate School of Public Administration) and Brenda Kübler-Mabbott*

**For further information regarding the series, please contact:**

Craig Fowlie, Publisher, Politics & International Studies
Taylor & Francis
2 Park Square, Milton Park, Abingdon
Oxford OX14 4RN, UK

+44 (0)207 842 2057 Tel
+44 (0)207 842 2302 Fax

Craig.Fowlie@tandf.co.uk
www.routledge.com

# The North Atlantic Treaty Organization
## The Enduring Alliance

**Julian Lindley-French**

 Routledge
Taylor & Francis Group

LONDON AND NEW YORK

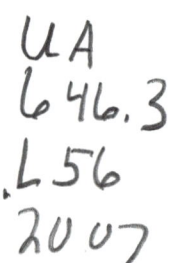

First published 2007 by Routledge
2 Park Square, Milton Park, Abingdon, Oxon OX14 4RN

Simultaneously published in the USA and Canada
by Routledge
270 Madison Ave, New York NY 10016

*Routledge is an imprint of the Taylor & Francis Group, an informa business*

© 2007 Julian Lindley-French

Typeset in Times New Roman by
Taylor & Francis Books
Printed and bound in Great Britain by
TJ International Ltd, Padstow, Cornwall

*British Library Cataloguing in Publication Data*
A catalogue record for this book is available from the British Library

*Library of Congress Cataloging in Publication Data*
A catalog record for this title has been requested

ISBN10: 0-415-35880-9  ISBN13: 978-0-415-35880-4 (pbk)
ISBN10: 0-415-35879-5  ISBN13: 978-0-415-35879-8 (hbk)

For Corine

# Contents

# Foreword

The current volume is the ninth in a new and dynamic series on "global institutions." The series strives (and, based on the initial volumes we believe, it succeeds) to provide readers with definitive guides to the most visible aspects of what we know as "global governance." Remarkable as it may seem, there exist relatively few books that offer in-depth treatments of prominent global bodies and processes, much less an entire series of concise and complementary volumes. Those that do exist are either out of date, inaccessible to the non-specialist reader, or seek to develop a specialized understanding of particular aspects of an institution or process rather than offer an overall account of its functioning. Similarly, existing books have often been written in highly technical language or have been crafted "in-house" and are notoriously self-serving and narrow.

The advent of electronic media has helped by making information, documents, and the resolutions of international organizations more widely available, but it has also complicated matters. The growing reliance on the Internet and other electronic methods of finding information about key international organizations and processes has served, ironically, to limit the educational materials to which most readers have ready access – namely, books. Public relations documents, raw data, and loosely refereed websites do not make for intelligent analysis. Official publications compete with a vast amount of electronically available information, much of which is suspect because of its ideological or self-promoting slant. Paradoxically, the growing range of purportedly independent websites offering analyses of the activities of particular organizations have emerged, but one inadvertent consequence has been to frustrate access to basic, authoritative, critical, and well-researched texts. The market for such has actually been reduced by the ready availability of varying quality electronic materials.

For those of us that teach, research, and practice in the area, this access to information has been at best frustrating. We were delighted, then, when Routledge saw the value of a series that bucks this trend and provides key reference points to the most significant global institutions. They are betting that serious students and professionals will want serious analyses. We have assembled a first-rate line-up of authors to address that market. Our intention, then, is to provide one-stop shopping for all readers – students (both undergraduate and postgraduate), interested negotiators, diplomats, practitioners from nongovernmental and intergovernmental organizations, and interested parties alike – seeking information about the most prominent institutional aspects of global governance.

## The North Atlantic Treaty Organization

When we first sat down to think about the line-up for our series on "global" institutions, we nonetheless placed very high on our list of priorities a book about an institution that was not global in membership or reach – NATO, the most powerful alliance composed only of Western countries. Founded in 1949 primarily to counter the perceived military threat from the Soviet Union and its allies, NATO members agreed in its oft-cited Article 5 that an attack on one of them would be considered as an attack against them all. Originally consisting of twelve members, it was increased by three more in the 1950s, including West Germany. The Soviet Union responded by establishing the Warsaw Pact in 1955. The Alliance was so successful as a deterrent that it never resorted to Article 5 or deployed the substantial military forces under its umbrella during the Cold War.

The fall of the Berlin Wall in 1989 and the implosion of the Soviet Union and the Warsaw Pact in 1991 led to a reassessment of the Alliance's role in the world. One clear need was to keep the non-European members, and especially the United States, engaged in Europe. Another was to reassess NATO's role in relationship to the erstwhile Soviet bloc. A third was to find a new diplomatic and military role for the Alliance.

Fifty-five years after its foundation, the Alliance invited formerly communist states (but not Russia) to join the partnership for peace, and in February 1994 launched its first-ever aggressive military operation in Bosnia-Herzegovina when it shot down Serbian fighter planes violating a UN "no-fly zone" and also bombed Serbian ground targets. In 1997 Russia gained a formal voice in NATO's affairs in return for the acceptance of an expansion into Eastern Europe. At present,

NATO has twenty-six members including several former Soviet allies. And in 1999, NATO engaged in a humanitarian war in Kosovo, and has subsequently been involved in training and other military activities in Afghanistan.

NATO has twenty countries associated with its Partnership for Peace (including twelve former Soviet Republics), and is engaged in the Mediterranean Dialogue with another seven countries from the southern side of the Mediterranean. American dominance of the institution has always been a reality – leading to the departure of France from the institution in 1966 and the subsequent departure of the Supreme Headquarters Allied Powers Europe (SHAPE) from Paris to Brussels in 1967.

The adaptation and transformation of institutions is a common thread in this series, and nowhere is this more obvious than with NATO. What a ride it has been! When we thought about possible authors, Julian Lindley-French's name jumped immediately to mind. Currently a senior scholar at the Center for Applied Policy at the University of Munich, and Senior Associate Fellow at the Defence Academy of the United Kingdom, Julian is a well-published commentator on transatlantic relations and European security and defense. As the historical nuts-and-bolts of the Western Alliance are essential to understanding its past and thinking about its future, we recommend to readers his authoritative 2005 work *A Chronology of European Security and Defence 1945–2005*.[1] Julian has acted as a consultant to NATO and lectured widely on transatlantic relations and European defense including at the Department of War Studies, King's College London, at the European Union Institute for Security Studies in Paris, and at the Geneva Center for Security Policy.

We have come to trust our authors; Julian is no different. We were delighted when he accepted our offer to contribute this book to the series; and we are proud of the result. He has produced an insightful volume that charts a path through the congested terrain of the Cold War and post-Cold War periods, including current concerns such as fighting terrorism and halting the proliferation of weapons of mass destruction. It is a first-rate book: informative, knowledgeable, and considered – with a dose of amusing anecdotes as well. We know those who have come to expect the highest standards from our books will not be disappointed. We are pleased to recommend it to all. As always, comments and suggestions from readers are welcome.

Thomas G. Weiss, The CUNY Graduate Center, New York, USA
Rorden Wilkinson, University of Manchester, UK
May 2006

# List of Acronyms

| | |
|---|---|
| ABM | Anti-Ballistic Missile (treaty) |
| ACO | Allied Command Operations |
| ACT | Allied Command Transformation |
| ACTORD | Action Order |
| AFNORTH | Allied Forces North |
| AFSOUTH | Allied Forces South |
| AJP | Allied Joint Publications |
| AMD | Allied Missile Defense |
| ANF | Atlantic Nuclear Force |
| AP | Allied Publications |
| ARRC | Allied Command Europe, Rapid Reaction Corps |
| ASEAN | Association of South-East Asian Nations |
| ATA | Atlantic Treaty Association |
| AU | African Union |
| AWAC | Airborne Warning and Control |
| BAOR | British Army of the Rhine |
| BG | Battle Groups |
| B-29 | American Long-Range Bomber |
| CAT | Crisis Action Team |
| CBRN | Chemical, Biological, Radiological and Nuclear |
| CEDP | Common European Defense Policy |
| CESDP | Common European Security and Defense Policy |
| C4 | Command, Control, Communications and Computers |
| CFE | Conventional Armed Forces in Europe (talks/treaty) |
| CFSP | Common Foreign and Security Policy |
| CHOD | Chiefs of Defense Staff |
| CIMIC | Civil Military Co-operation |
| CIS | Commonwealth of Independent States |
| CJPS | Combined Joint Planning Staffs |

| CJTF | Combined Joint Task Force |
| COMUSEUCOM | Commander of the US European Command |
| CPSU | Communist Party of the Soviet Union |
| CRO | Crisis Response Operation |
| CSCE | Conference on Security and Co-operation in Europe |
| DCI | Defense Capabilities Initiative |
| DPC | Defense Planning Committee |
| DPKO | Department of Peacekeeping Operations (UN) |
| DPP | Defense Planning Process |
| DSACEUR | Deputy Supreme Allied Commander, Europe |
| DSACT | Deputy Supreme Allied Commander, Transformation |
| EAPC | Euro-Atlantic Partnership Council |
| EC | European Community |
| ECAP | European Capabilities Action Plan |
| ECSC | European Coal and Steel Community |
| EDC | European Defense Community |
| EDU | European Defense Union |
| EEC | European Economic Community |
| EPC | European Political Co-operation |
| ERRC | European Rapid Reaction Corps |
| ERRF | European Rapid Reaction Force |
| ERRM | European Rapid Reaction Mechanism |
| ESDI | European Security and Defense Identity |
| ESDP | European Security and Defense Policy |
| ESS | European Security Strategy |
| EU | European Union |
| EUFOR | EU Force |
| EUMC | EU Military Committee |
| EUROFOR | European Force |
| EUROMARFOR | European Maritime Force |
| FAWEU | Forces Answerable to the Western European Union |
| FBEAG | Franco-British European Air Group |
| FBS | Forward Base System |
| FLR | Forces of Lower Readiness |
| FOC | Full Operating Capability |
| FOFA | Follow-on Force Attack |
| FRG | Federal Republic of Germany |
| FYROM | Former Yugoslav Republic of Macedonia |
| GAC | General Affairs Council |
| GDP | Gross Domestic Product |
| GDR | German Democratic Republic |
| GLCM | Ground-Launched Cruise Missile |

| | |
|---|---|
| GPALS | Global Protection Against Limited Strikes |
| GSFG | Group of Soviet Forces Germany |
| GWOT | Global War on Terror |
| HG2010 | Headline Goal 2010 |
| HHG | Helsinki Headline Goal |
| HLG | High-Level Group |
| HQ COMSPMARFOR | HQ Commander Spanish Maritime Forces |
| HQ COMUKMARFOR | HQ Commander UK Maritime Forces |
| HRF | High-Readiness Forces |
| IAEA | International Atomic Energy Agency |
| ICBM | Intercontinental Ballistic Missile |
| ICI | Istanbul Co-operation Initiative |
| IEPG | Independent European Program Group |
| IFOR | Implementation Force |
| IGC | Intergovernmental Conference |
| IISS | International Institute for Strategic Studies |
| IMS | Integrated Military Structure |
| INF | Intermediate Nuclear Forces |
| IO | International Organization |
| IPP | Individual Partnership Program |
| IPSC | Interim Political and Security Committee |
| IPTF | International Police Task Force |
| IS | International Staff |
| ISA | International Security Assistance Force |
| ISTAR | Intelligence, Surveillance, Target Acquisition & Reconnaissance |
| JNA | Yugoslav National Army |
| KFOR | Kosovo Force |
| LRTNF | Long-Range Theater Nuclear Forces |
| LTDP | Long-Term Defense Program |
| MAD | Mutually Assured Destruction |
| MAP | Membership Action Plan |
| MAPEX | Map Exercise |
| MBFR | Mutually Balanced Force Reduction |
| MC | Military Committee |
| MIRV | Multiple Independent Re-entry Vehicle |
| MIT | Military Implications Team |
| MLF | Multilateral Force |
| MRCA | Multi-role Combat Aircraft |
| NAC | North Atlantic Council |
| NACC | North Atlantic Co-operation Council |
| NATO | North Atlantic Treaty Organization |

| | |
|---|---|
| NATO PA | NATO Parliamentary Assembly |
| NBC | Nuclear, Biological and Chemical |
| NCS | NATO Command Structure |
| NCW | Network-centric Warfare |
| NFS | NATO Force Structure |
| NGO | Non-Governmental Organization |
| NPG | Nuclear Planning Group |
| NRF | NATO Response Force |
| NSC | National Security Council |
| NSC | New Strategic Concept |
| NSDD | National Security Decision Directive |
| NSDM | National Security Decision Memorandum |
| NSF | NATO Security Force |
| NST | Nuclear and Space Talks |
| N3CA | NATO Consultation, Command and Control Agency |
| NURC | NATO Undersea Research Center |
| OEF | Operation Enduring Freedom |
| OPEC | Organization of Petroleum-Exporting Countries |
| ORBAT | Order of Battle |
| OSCE | Organization for Security and Co-operation in Europe |
| PARP | Partnership Planning and Review Process |
| PC | Political Committee |
| PCC | Prague Capabilities Commitment |
| PCG | Policy Co-ordination Group |
| PD | Presidential Directive |
| PfP | Partnership for Peace |
| PGM | Precision-Guided Munitions |
| PIT | Political Implications Team |
| PJC | NATO–Russia Permanent Joint Council |
| PJHQ | Permanent Joint Headquarters |
| PRT | Provincial Reconstruction Team |
| PSC | Political and Security Committee |
| PSO | Peace Support Operation |
| QDR | Quadrennial Defense Review |
| R&T | Research and Technology |
| RHQ AFNORTH | Regional Headquarters, Allied Forces North |
| RMA | Revolution in Military Affairs |
| RSFSR | Russian Soviet Federal Socialist Republic |
| RTA | Research and Technology Agency |
| SACEUR | Supreme Allied Commander, Europe |
| SACT | Supreme Allied Commander, Transformation |

| | |
|---|---|
| SALT | Strategic Arms Limitation Talks |
| SCEPC | Senior Civil Emergency Planning Committee |
| SDI | Strategic Defense Initiative |
| SEAD | Suppression of Enemy Air Defenses |
| SEATO | South East Asia Treaty Organization |
| SED | East German Communist Party |
| SFOR | Stabilization Force |
| SHAPE | Supreme Headquarters Allied Powers Europe |
| SITCEN | Situation Center |
| SOF | Special Operations Forces |
| SPC | Senior Political Committee |
| SRF | Strategic Rocket Force |
| SS | Surface to Surface Missile (Soviet) |
| SSBN | Submersible Ballistic Nuclear |
| SSM | Surface to Surface Missile (Western) |
| STANAVLANT | Standing Naval Force, Atlantic |
| STANAVFORMED | Standing Naval Force, Mediterranean |
| START | Strategic Arms Reduction Talks |
| TEU | Treaty on European Union |
| TNF | Theater Nuclear Forces |
| UK | United Kingdom |
| UKNAF | UK–Netherlands Amphibious Force |
| UN | United Nations |
| UNMIBH | United Nations Mission in Bosnia and Herzegovina |
| UNPA | United Nations Protected Areas |
| UNPROFOR | United Nations Protection Force |
| UNSC | United Nations Security Council |
| UNSCOM | United Nations Special Commission |
| US | United States |
| USSR | Union of Soviet Socialist Republics |
| VHF | Very High Readiness Forces |
| WEAG | Western European Armaments Group |
| WEU | Western European Union |
| WMD | Weapons of Mass Destruction |
| WTO | Warsaw Treaty Organization |

# Introduction

- Five Core Messages
- The North Atlantic Treaty Organization: The Enduring Alliance

There is an irreverent joke that it is illuminating to consider. NATO Secretary-General, Jaap de Hoop Scheffer, and EU High Representative, Javier Solana, are having breakfast with God. Conversation tilts this way and that in a spirit of camaraderie and good humor. Towards the end of breakfast de Hoop Scheffer puts a direct question to the all-powerful, all-seeing one. "Tell me, God, will NATO ever be a truly global security and defense organization?" God thinks hard about this question and after some reflection replies, "Yes, Jaap, but not in *your* lifetime." Javier Solana, not to be outdone and having much experience of both NATO and the EU, poses a similar question. "God, will the EU ever be a functioning security and defense organization?" At first God looks baffled, and then worried, and after a seeming eternity replies: "Yes, Javier, but not in *my* lifetime." That mythical exchange captures at least part of NATO's reality (as it does the EU's) as the organization takes on new roles in a new world. The central question posed by this book is: can NATO close the gap between the politico-military challenges the Allies face and the politico-military power it can generate? The central message of this book is that is precisely the challenge NATO has always faced, and indeed will face.

Today NATO has twenty-six members: Belgium, Bulgaria, Canada, the Czech Republic, Denmark, Estonia, France, Germany, Greece, Hungary, Iceland, Italy, Latvia, Lithuania, Luxembourg, the Netherlands, Norway, Poland, Portugal, Romania, Slovakia, Slovenia, Spain, Turkey, the United Kingdom and the United States. And, it is a testament to the political value of the Alliance that ten of those countries were members of the Warsaw Treaty Organization, NATO's adversary.

Ever since its creation in 1949 the North Atlantic Treaty Organization (NATO) has been an organization that has been asked to do too much, with too little, with members from very different strategic backgrounds and cultures. Such different traditions have led to very different strategic visions with which the Alliance has had to cope. Throughout the Cold War, Americans sought to maintain continental American invulnerability, whereas Europeans saw vulnerability as simply a fact of life. Americans saw security and defense as intrinsically linked to their own idea, Europeans saw security and defense as intrinsically linked to where they lived. Americans saw the Cold War as a global struggle, Europeans as simply the latest chapter in the European power struggle down the ages. Americans were containing Soviet communism, Europeans were confronting Russians. Europeans were in retreat from global leadership, Americans were preparing for it. It was, and is, ever thus.

Today, as NATO embarks on new missions it faces a world in which the very nature and utility of power is being questioned. For all that, NATO's story is one of success. That the Alliance made the major contribution in winning the Cold War cannot be questioned. The political solidarity of democracies is an awesome weapon when credible and cohesive, a fact that should not be lost on those seeking to challenge the West.

Equally, NATO is a "big security" organization that is at its best dealing with "big picture" security. Consequently, as an extension of the transatlantic security relationship that it serves, NATO has never been particularly comfortable, or successful, when dealing with "small picture" security. The sub-strategic conflict of the type that tragically ground its way across the Balkans in the 1990s challenged not just Europe, but the very utility of political tools such as NATO. Indeed, like its political masters, NATO struggled to find a solution to a war that was of a state, rather than between states. The Wars of the Yugoslav Succession demonstrated the difficulties the Alliance has confronted as it moved away from classical confrontation à la Cold War, through the strategic vacation of the 1990s, en route to the strategic stabilization missions of NATO's future.

Consequently, this book is about NATO's past, present and future because an understanding of all three is essential to answer the question at the heart of this study: why NATO endures. It is thus about NATO's place in a new world in which big picture security is slowly, but inexorably, beginning to re-assert itself. The mantras of the 1990s and the first decade of this century that can be found in NATO's Strategic Concept – terrorism, weapons of mass destruction, state failure, regional conflict, instability *et al.* – remain dangerous and compelling security challenges. However, they are today being replaced by something that the Founding Fathers of NATO, Dean Acheson, Ernest Bevin and Robert Schuman, would have well understood back in the 1940s.

The age of post 9/11–Iraq big picture politics that the world is entering with the emergence of an Asia fueled by rapid but unstable growth, allied to the missed opportunity for Western leadership of the 1990s, will lead inexorably to the return of a big NATO. NATO started its life as a European organization, it is about to embark on a new life as the world's first truly global military security organization.

## Five Core Messages

There are five core messages:
- Strategic counter-terror is mutating: The strategic manhunt of the immediate post-9/11 period, reminiscent of the Old Wild West, is over. It would be good to capture Osama bin Laden and his cohorts but they are but bit-part actors. Behind their mask of intolerance and hatred the West has discovered a new Thirty Years War that will take sustained engagement across the political, economic, diplomatic and military spectrum in the total security age of the twenty-first century.
- New power and new threats are emerging: The threats are developing driven by the intense change that is taking place in Asia. In many ways, the twenty-first century will be Asia's age. Like that of Europe before it, Asia's emergence is unlikely to proceed smoothly. There will be *scarums* and *alarums* until Asian power is properly embedded in the great institutions the West built. Until then a balanced transatlantic relationship will remain the world's most important insurance mechanism against the political consequences of uncontrolled and extra-institutional change.
- Security globalization requires visionary security governance: The connectivity that is globalization is throwing up a host of global challenges that were once only regional, of "haves" and "have nots," of the connected and unconnected. The West must cope with it.
- NATO must plan for a total security age: Article 5 still matters. Indeed, the political stability and ongoing political development of new Alliance members rests upon the stability that both NATO and the EU afford them. It matters also for Moscow. The Euro-Atlantic area represents the only stable border that Russia has in this dangerous world. Indeed, in a world so electronically independent, as borders become virtual disruption could be akin to destruction for societies so dependent on critical infrastructures. NATO needs new partners and new tools.

• Democratic military power has its limits, but is still vital: So many of the threats faced are non-traditional, such as global warming, pandemics etc. The West must shape old and new institutions to engage such challenges. At the same time, the world is not so different from that of the past. Credible, legitimate military power and effective organization still provides the bedrock of effective security governance.

## The North Atlantic Treaty Organization: The Enduring Alliance

*The North Atlantic Treaty Organization: The Enduring Alliance* looks beyond the splits in the Alliance and goes back to the roots of NATO's past to paint a big security picture and of NATO's role therein. The book deals with all the fundamentals: history, structure, policy, capability and change, but its natural center of gravity is the strategic vision that underpins the political cohesion that makes NATO what it is. The book therefore places NATO in the context of the change that has taken place over the years. In other words, this book is about the what, the why, the how, the when and the what-next of NATO.

The book is divided into three main sections: Cold War NATO, Strategic Vacation, and New Age NATO.

Chapter 1, "A World Gone Mad: 9/11 and Iraq," sets the scene. It explores the Alliance in the aftermath of the attacks on New York and Washington on 11 September 2001, as Americans go to war, and Europeans do not. It considers the challenges of going to Afghanistan and delves into the politics of confrontation within the Alliance as Old Atlantic confronts Old Europe in the run-up to the Iraq War, in the midst of the search for the new strategic consensus. It assesses the sheer scale of the challenges posed by the Global War on Terror and contrasts NATO's new missions with those given it by the Founding Fathers.

Chapter 2, "Facing the Enemy," demonstrates that crises, both internal and external, have provided an essential political tension within the Alliance that has driven change therein. The chapter undertakes an in-depth analysis of the events and people that shaped NATO from its very origins at the close of World War Two to the dawn of détente. It follows NATO as it grapples with a series of crises, from the Berlin airlift that created it, through the European Defense Community, the Missile Gap, France's withdrawal from military NATO, and the establishment of the direct superpower dialog.

Chapter 3, "Coping with the Allies," explores the widening gap between Americans and Europeans in the second half of the Cold War, and explains why the many arguments that infused NATO represented the very pluralism that gave this multi-voiced democratic security community its essential strength. From the splits of the 1973 Yom Kippur War, through the Euromissiles crisis that spanned the 1970s and 1980s, emerging European integration, and on to eventual victory, NATO was the essential platform for solidarity, the shield of democracy and the mechanism for internal crisis management.

Chapter 4, "Strategic Vacation," considers why NATO endured having completed the mission for which it was created, even as it searched for a new role. The chapter looks at the challenges posed by the end of the Cold War and the many contradictions victory generated for NATO, as defense was cut even as Yugoslavia collapsed. It also looks at the relationship with the emerging Europe as NATO and what would become the European Union began a long and difficult journey to find an accommodation acceptable to all members of both institutions.

Chapter 5, "The Search for a New Strategic Consensus," explores the search for strategic consensus in a world that was slowly beginning to regain strategic shape. The chapter considers the impact of over-militarized American security policy and over-civilianized European security policy on the Alliance, together with the slow realization that new dangers would bring the strategic vacation to an end.

Chapter 6, "NATO Today," examines the structure, working and people of the Alliance and considers recent reforms as the chapter assesses the challenges that NATO faces. It looks at the state of Alliance armed forces, the difficulties Europeans face in developing sufficient hard military capabilities, and the unease of Americans when engaged in nation-building. The chapter also considers the lessons learned thus far from Afghanistan and Iraq and why only the Alliance can act as the global strategic enabler that brings legitimacy and effectiveness together.

Finally, Chapter 7, "The Past, Present and Future of NATO," brings all three phases of the Alliance's life together and offers a broad view of its future in a complex world in which the challenge of terrorism and instability co-exist with the return of great power and geopolitics. The chapter brings NATO's story full circle; having been created to preserve the security of its members in the face of an overwhelming threat, the Alliance must once again grapple with the challenge of how best to organize democratic societies and free peoples forced to confront the dangerous world into which they are moving.

This, then, is the story of *NATO: The Enduring Alliance*.

# 1 A World Gone Mad: 9/11 and Iraq

- The Invoking of Article 5
- The End of the Out of Area Debate
- The Global War on Terror and the Re-emergence of Russia
- NATO and the Axis of Evil
- Old Atlantic versus Old Europe
- The Re-building of the Alliance
- European Security Strategy and Istanbul: Looking to the Future

> . . . states like these [North Korea, Iraq and Iran], and their terrorist allies, constitute an axis of evil, aiming to threaten the peace of the world.
>
> President George W. Bush, State of the Union Address, 29 January 2002[1]

It is 11 September 2001. The morning rush hour is coming to its bustling end on the highways, byways and subways of New York. High up in the twin towers of the World Trade Center people are settling down to work as the New York financial and legal center gets into its stride. Suddenly, at 8:46 a.m., as if from nowhere, an American Airlines Boeing 767 slams into the North Tower. Al Qaeda has begun its day of carnage. Two hours later over 3000 people are dead, the twin towers are no more, and parts of the Pentagon and Pennsylvania smolder with the wreckage of hatred, fundamentalism and terror. In a few moments NATO's world and its relationships are changed forever. It is the beginning of the end of European isolationism. It is the end of the beginning of American unilateralism. It is also the beginning of a new, big NATO, as strategic terror, state failure and the proliferation of weapons of mass destruction combine with the re-emergence of Russia and China and rogue states to create NATO's new world. A strategic cocktail that is given added spice by the clash of Western civilizations;

as American unilateralism confronts European institutionalism. It is a world gone mad. Big security has returned.

## The Invoking of Article 5

On 12 September 2001 what would have been unthinkable during the Cold War comes to pass. The North Atlantic Council (NAC) meets in emergency session to invoke Article 5. Only fifteen years before such a decision would have presaged nuclear Armageddon. Technically, NATO is on the verge of war – but against whom or what? That is to be the essential dilemma of struggle in the first decade of the twenty-first century. Equally, the invoking of Article 5 is the clearest indication yet that the world is once again a very big place.

Whilst the US welcomes the support of its Allies, Washington is too busy preparing to fight the Global War on Terror (GWOT). Suddenly, the small security that has dominated so much of Europe's isolationism since the end of the Cold War seems precisely that – small. Overnight, the prospect of strategic terrorists, armed by fanatical beliefs and even weapons of mass destruction, seems nightmarishly close. Al Qaeda, in one devastating action, affronts the US with the first lethal attack on its soil by a foreign force on Continental North America since 1812.[2] Americans go to war, Europeans do not.

Equally, European support for America is genuine and heartfelt. The French newspaper *Le Monde*, in its editorial on 12 September, proclaims, "We are all Americans."[3] Europeans collectively believe that. That same day, the UN Security Council adopts Resolution 1368 recognizing terrorism as a " . . . threat to international peace and security." And, on 21 September, at an extraordinary session of the European Council, the EU states that "The fight against terrorism will, more than ever, be a priority objective of the European Union."[4] All the tensions and suspicions between Americans and many Europeans that had so scarred the preceding years, evaporate in the face of the new challenge.

Indeed, the Global War on Terror leads to a series of firsts. On 4 October, NATO responds positively to a US request for support, even though the Alliance is at best marginal in America's response. On 7 October, following the refusal of the Taliban Government in Kabul to surrender Osama bin Laden and other senior Al Qaeda members, the US, UK, France, Australia, Canada and Germany begin Operation Enduring Freedom (OEF) against Afghanistan. On 9 October, NATO launches Operation Eagle Assist by sending five early-warning (AWAC) aircraft to monitor the skies over North America. It is the first time that NATO assets have been deployed in defense of continental North America.[5] On 26 October, NATO deploys naval forces (STANAVFORMED) to the eastern Mediterranean as part of counter-terrorism operations to monitor shipping, and on 25 November, US troops move into southern Afghanistan alongside coalition forces from twelve NATO and non-NATO partners. Notably, it is the first time since World War Two that German forces have embarked on combat operations outside Europe. Kabul falls soon after.

NATO has a vital role to play. From the outset it is clear that the US and its European Allies are going to be in Afghanistan for a long time, something for which Europeans had neither countenanced, nor prepared. On 22 December, the Interim Authority for Afghanistan is established under UN auspices, and the participants request the United Nations Security Council to authorize the early deployment to Afghanistan of a United Nations mandated force, to assist in the maintenance of security in Kabul and its surrounding areas, that in time could be expanded to other areas. What is to become one of NATO's most challenging missions is born – the International Security Assistance Force (ISAF). NATO is truly in the global security business.

The clock starts ticking. On 18 December, NATO defense ministers meet to discuss how to conduct the Global War on Terror, with particular emphasis on improving NATO's ability to project its forces world-wide. On 20 December, the UN Security Council authorizes the establishment of ISAF and on 21 December, the first British troops arrive in Afghanistan to prepare the ground. It is the first time in a century that British troops have entered the country in force. On 10 January 2002, the UK officially assumes command of ISAF.

## The End of the Out of Area Debate

For much of the 1990s NATO had been locked in a debate as to whether the Alliance should provide security and defense only on the territory of its members, or go beyond it. 9/11 ends the so-called out of area debate once and for all because if NATO is unable to play a role in American security then the Alliance has little or no future. Given the nature and the source of the challenge NATO must necessarily go global. Having agreed to do something is one thing; being able to do it is something else. Afghanistan reveals the extent of the dilemma Europeans face. At the end of the Cold War, the force-planning assumption of most Europeans was that they would not have to conduct major operations within Europe, let alone beyond it. There had been signs to the contrary that, by and large, they chose to ignore. Iraq, East Timor, Sierra Leone were but examples of a host of deployments beyond Europe that Europeans had undertaken since the end of the Cold War. Now they had to go in strength to Afghanistan, where the Soviets had been defeated in the 1980s, and where only the Maxim gun and Imperial "nous" had afforded the British "control" at the height of the British Empire in the nineteenth century. Put simply, Afghanistan was just about the least likely place for Europeans to deploy; and the most unwelcome. NATO had just entered a whole new ball game.

The Europeans face their perennial dilemma – how best to organize not enough capability in pursuit of far too much actuality. In some respects, the EU is better placed to organize the defense of Europe against terrorism than NATO, but NATO remains the essential platform for the projection of force, coercion and stabilization for anything but the most parochial of operations, and Afghanistan is most definitely not parochial. That said, the war on terror raises questions the Soviet Union never posed, not least the role of armed forces in such a struggle. On 19 October, that point is brought home, at a meeting of EU leaders in Ghent, Belgium, as a declaration is issued on the fight against terrorism and a "Road Map" is announced including moves towards a common arrest warrant, a common definition of terrorism, as well as anti-money laundering measures. They also agree on increased co-operation between key European agencies involved in the fight: Europol, Eurojust and the intelligence agencies of member-states. It is also apparent at the meeting the degree to which key EU member-states disagree with each other and the US over Washington's conduct of the Global War on Terror.

On 19–20 November, EU foreign and defense ministers meet in Brussels to discuss all-important military capability improvements. They agree a European Capabilities Action Plan (ECAP), separate from NATO's Defense Capabilities Initiative (DCI), to remedy fifty-five identified shortcomings in European military capabilities. Whilst co-operation with NATO is agreed, it is not central to the ECAP, which raises the prospect that NATO and EU efforts in the enhancement of capabilities will become disjointed.

However, although 9/11 and Afghanistan at one level exacerbate and accelerate transatlantic divergence, the seriousness of the situation does at least inject a new realism into European defense. At the European Council meeting in Laeken, Belgium, on 14–15 December, leaders agree that "To enable the European Union to carry out crisis management operations over the whole range of the Petersberg Tasks ... substantial progress is to be made." Key to this is EU–NATO agreement. Interestingly, invoking memories of Europe's first and failed attempt at defense integration in the 1950s, the European Defense Community, EU leaders assert that the proposed European Rapid Reaction Force (ERRF) " . . . does not imply the creation of a European Army."[6]

## The Global War on Terror and the Re-emergence of Russia

9/11 again changes the relationship with the old enemy, Russia. For over a decade Russia wallowed in post-Cold War decline, and was but a shadow of its former self. However, in Vladimir Putin it has a young President who understands the game of power politics and wants to play it. Two factors help the Russian cause. First, 9/11 increases tensions between the West and much of the Middle East, and Russia has plenty of energy to offer an energy-hungry West. Second, in President Bush, Putin has a like-minded counterpart. Moreover, Russia is fighting its own "terrorist" war in Chechnya against Islamic separatists, albeit in a brutal and ineffective manner.

However, Russia is a sensitive partner. Moscow felt humiliated during the Kosovo war in 1999 and was not going to allow itself to be marginalized again. Consequently, Russian foreign policy in the early part of the new decade is re-cast, founded upon the consolidation of internal power in the hands of the Kremlin, and the application of external influence through classical trade-offs with the West. Russia needs the West, NATO after all offers Moscow the one stable border it has, but Russia is going to exact a price for its co-operation in the Global War on Terror. It is a complex policy because Islamic fundamentalism poses as much of a threat to Russia as it poses to the West. Indeed, few recall that the reason for the Soviet invasion of Afghanistan back in 1979 was the danger posed by Islamic fundamentalism to its southern republics, and that Al Qaeda grew out of the struggle against Soviet forces there. However, Putin concludes that Russia's strategic location and critical mass affords Moscow a role on which it can re-build a strategic relationship with the US, a standing Russian obsession. As during the Cold War, the main point of political contention is the purpose, shape and structure of NATO.

In the immediate wake of 9/11 Russia offers America both solidarity and support. On 13 September, the NATO–Russia Permanent Joint Council issues a statement condemning the attacks. On 3 October, Putin surprisingly suggests that Russia will not oppose NATO enlargement to the Baltic States, citing growing Russia–NATO co-operation. Moreover, on 7 December 2001, NATO foreign ministers announce a new, beefed-up NATO–Russia Council to strengthen ties with Moscow, in order to smooth the Alliance's further enlargement, and as a recognition of the new realities. But there are limits. Russia also seeks a *de facto* veto over Alliance activities. Not unexpectedly the Alliance refuses. Moreover, on 13 December, President Bush announces the withdrawal of the US from the 1972 ABM Treaty to pave the way for the development of an anti-ballistic missile defense shield for continental US that becomes known simply as Missile Defense. Whilst Putin says the move does not pose a threat to Russia, he calls the decision a mistake, and calls for the rapid creation of a new framework for the US–Russian strategic relationship. The Cold War architecture is being re-cast.

On cue, in an event rich in Cold War tradition, on 23–24 May 2002, US President George W. Bush and Russian President Vladimir Putin sign the Treaty of Moscow, reducing stockpiles of nuclear weapons by two-thirds over ten years, and agreeing to co-operate on energy policy and counter-terrorism. It is the end of the SALT–START process that first began way back in 1972; and the start of Russia's strategic rehabilitation. Four days later, at the first meeting of the NATO–Russia Council, it is stressed that Russia and NATO member-nations will work as equal partners in areas of common interest.

## NATO and the Axis of Evil

Above all, 9/11 puts the transatlantic relationship in a new strategic context. On 29 January 2002, President Bush, in his State of the Union address, attacks North Korea, Iran and Iraq. It is the birth of the Bush Doctrine and US unilateralism. NATO is put on notice. On 1–3 February, US Deputy Secretary of Defense, Paul Wolfowitz, states, " . . . the mission must determine the coalition," and not vice versa. Otherwise, " . . . the coalition is reduced to the lowest common denominator."[7] In a sense, the Bush Doctrine is a re-hash of Mikhail Gorbachev's Sinatra Doctrine at the end of the 1990s – the US is going to do it "My Way."[8]

The immediate reactions are twofold. On the one hand, some fear the end of the transatlantic relationship as strategic divergence widens. On the other, Europeans endeavor to convince Washington that their support for the Global War on Terror makes them worthy partners and must be listened to. Indeed, there is much that should keep Europeans and Americans focused on a successful relationship. However, whilst the US goes global, much of Europe remains stubbornly regional. This accelerates the transfer of political security authority from NATO to the EU within Europe, not least because there are serious questions concerning US commitment to the Alliance. To that end, on 15–16 March, the Barcelona European Council of the

EU declares that the EU is "available" to take over NATO's operation in Macedonia, " ... on the understanding that the permanent arrangements on EU–NATO co-operation (known as Berlin-plus) would be in place by then."9

On 30 April, EU High Representative, Javier Solana, and NATO Secretary-General, Lord Robertson, meet for the first time at NATO Headquarters to discuss NATO–EU co-operation, which is followed by another meeting on 25 June to discuss NATO and EU contributions towards the Global War on Terror, the situation in the Balkans and progress on EU access to NATO assets and capabilities. On 14–15 May, NATO and EU foreign ministers meet in Iceland to discuss the use of Alliance assets and capabilities by the EU. Little progress is made.

## Old Atlantic versus Old Europe

And then comes Iraq. In April 2002, on the eve of the US–UK Crawford Summit, Tony Blair gives a speech in the US that outlines a new doctrine: strategic pre-emption. In an age of proliferation threats have to be dealt with before they materialize and Saddam Hussein represents just such a threat. Regime change is needed.10 Much of Europe demurs. It is taking the Global War on Terror just one step too far. By May, hard-line neoconservatives in Washington want to confront Saddam with or without a UN Security Council resolution authorizing such action. The neocons and US unilateralism not only marginalize international institutions, including NATO, but they also put the search for strategic consensus on hold. State power is where it is at, particularly American state power, and allies have to make a choice – either with us or against us. Thus, as Bush and Blair move closer over the need to confront Iraq, much of Europe runs for cover. It is of little surprise that France and Germany also move closer in opposition. The Alliance is on the brink, arguably, of its greatest ever split.

But Tony Blair cannot ignore the UN. He needs a UN Security Council Resolution to go to war and in September, President Bush agrees to give the UN route a further try, even if his resolve is apparent. On 17 September, Chancellor Gerhard Schroeder stages an impressive political rally to take the German elections, much of it on the back of anti-American, anti-war rhetoric. The Alliance is approaching a tipping point. It is a moment further complicated by the planned enlargements of both NATO and the EU. With the prospect of ten US-friendly powers joining both NATO and the Union, much to the benefit of London, France swings behind its old European partner Germany. France stands on an issue of principle, the weapons inspectors must be given due time, but Paris also calculates that damaging London will anchor the Franco-German axis at the center of an enlarged European Union. For Germany, in the midst of an election, and with much of the population against the use of force in any circumstances, an anti-war stance is good politics. In reality, both sides are playing power politics. It is a very European game, at a very strategic moment.

The return of great power politics is another consequence of 9/11. To such an extent that on 18 July 2002, Belgian Prime Minister, Guy Verhofstadt, warns that "the development of the [EUs] European Security and Defense Policy is not making sufficient progress," adding that " . . . over the past few months, I have perceived a risk of re-nationalization of defense policies . . . the danger persists, in my opinion, in seeing both the European Union and NATO turn into toolboxes for supporting ad hoc coalitions."[11] The plain fact is that the radicalization of US security policy, the institutionalization of European security, and the fact of American power leave many smaller Europeans trapped between loyalty to the US and the EU. In such circumstances the impact of any major split between the big powers is magnified, damaging both the Alliance and the EU. Unfortunately, Iraq takes place at a very particular moment in Europe's long development, as Europeans try to grasp the new post-9/11 reality.

Against that background, on 8 November, and after much wrangling between Washington, London, Paris, Berlin and Moscow, UN Security Council Resolution 1441 is passed, giving Iraq one final opportunity to comply with its international obligations. The UN Security Council warns Iraq it will face serious consequences if it continues to violate its obligations. However, the resolution stops short of explicitly authorizing force if Iraq continues in "material breach." It is a piece of constructive ambiguity that will soon trigger a near-death experience for the Alliance.

On 21 November 2002, French Foreign Minister, Dominique de Villepin, and German Foreign Minister, Joschka Fischer, call for common security and solidarity, between those member-states who wish to co-operate more closely with each other on defense. At the 40th anniversary of the Elysée Treaty in January 2003, France and Germany propose to develop the European Security and Defense Policy (ESDP) into a European Security and Defense Union; the rhetoric is as empty as the halls of Versailles through which it sails. On 29 April 2003, the same day as American forces take Baghdad, Belgium, Luxembourg, France and Germany agree to create a new rapid reaction force built around the Franco-German brigade. The timing could not have been more provocative. Even though there can be no serious European defense without the British, Europe's strongest military power, and no sustained serious operations without the US and NATO, the point is made.

Unfortunately, NATO is caught in the political crossfire. On 10 February 2003, Turkey invokes Article 4 of the North Atlantic Treaty, fearing that its " . . . territorial integrity, political independence or security . . . is threatened" by Baghdad as a consequence of the impending war in Iraq. Indeed, under Article 4, the Alliance consults whenever a member feels that its territorial integrity, political independence or security is threatened. However, France, Germany and Belgium refuse to begin planning for any such contingency on the grounds that such a move would be premature and would undermine UN efforts to resolve the crisis. And, it is only after Lord Robertson forces a decision through the Defense Planning Committee (DPC) is aid for Turkey approved. France, which had not been a member of the DPC since it withdrew in 1966, consequently finds itself out-maneuvered. With France sidelined, Germany drops its objections and Belgium soon follows suit. History has come full circle.

NATO is once again at a crossroads. Indeed, Iraq is not really about Iraq. Rather, it is about the future organization of power in Europe. France's perennial problem is that its vis ion for an autonomous European defense is founded on the weak Germans and not the strong British and the French know they can only push it so far. Moreover, all the missed opportunities of the 1990s to improve European foreign and security policy power come home to roost as those against a robust intervention in Iraq are left with little else but gesture politics.

## The Re-building of the Alliance

Equally, the consequences of the split over Iraq are not all negative. 9/11 and the Iraq War strip away the pretence and empty rhetoric of the 1990s and confront NATO members with the stark reality of their vulnerability as the first great age of the twenty-first century begins to unfold. Indeed, it is impressive, the speed at which the new strategic realities imposed by 9/11, overcome the split over Iraq. It also reminds Americans that in a complex world power is not enough. Power must be legitimate to be effective and other democracies afford the most important pool of legitimacy available. That NATO does not collapse has far more to do with emerging strategic realities of the twenty-first century than banal calls to shared values, but the shared democratic tradition does matter. By 2003 the world is beginning to take on a shape closer to the strategic challenge of the Cold War, than the bumbling strategic vacation of the 1990s. It is a world in which ever more destructive power cascades into the hands of ever smaller actors as the dark side of globalization wreaks its havoc. It is a world in which new great power jostles with old great power, much of it unembedded in security institutions, like NATO and the EU. It is a world in which the demands for energy create the conditions for renewed state competition. It is a world that is changing fast. Thankfully, every NATO member takes a step back from the abyss into which they briefly peered and realize how close they have come to destroying the West's priceless security asset – NATO.

Furthermore, even though the damage done to the Alliance, Europe and the West by the Iraq War is not to be underestimated, the strength of all three is also apparent. To an extent, most NATO and EU members are picking up the wreckage even as it is being created. On 21–22 November 2002, at NATO's Prague Summit, Bulgaria, Estonia, Latvia, Lithuania, Romania, Slovakia and Slovenia are invited to join the Alliance. To close the gap between military rhetoric and reality, the gathered NATO Heads of State and Government also replace the Defense Capabilities Initiative (DCI) with the more modest Prague Capabilities Commitment (PCC). The Allies also agree to set up the 21,000-strong NATO Response Force (NRF), as the spearhead of a robust NATO crisis management capability and to streamline the Alliance's command structure to emphasize the projection of capabilities, rather than the defense of territory. Interestingly, France is at the forefront of much of this good work.[12]

On 12–13 December 2002, EU leaders also indicate a willingness to take their European Security and Defense Policy (ESDP) to a new level by stating the " . . . Union's willingness to lead a military operation in Bosnia following SFOR [the NATO Stabilization Force]."[13] On 13 December, the North Atlantic Council gives the go-ahead for the advancement of all outstanding issues regarding EU–NATO relations. Finally, on 16 December, Robertson and Solana sign "The EU–NATO Declaration on ESDP," that provides for the "fullest possible involvement" of non-EU, NATO members in ESDP, in return for which the EU gains access to NATO planning, intelligence and logistics assets and capabilities after three years of difficult negotiations. Solana also declares that the EU will be ready by February 2003 to take over operations in Macedonia, and that the EU will look to take over NATO's SFOR mission in Bosnia with an EU Force (EUFOR) by the end of 2003.

Thus, behind the headlines a new pragmatism slowly emerges. The EU is to become the organizing locus of much of Europe's sub-strategic security, whilst NATO begins planning for the global strategic stabilization and hard defense missions that are its future. On 10 June 2003, the EU's Political and Security Committee adopt the "Basic Principles for an EU Strategy Against Proliferation of Weapons of Mass Destruction." On 12 June, the EU deploys to Congo to prevent genocide with the full backing of the UN Security Council, and on 25 June, at the transatlantic summit in Washington, NATO and the EU launch the "Joint Initiative Against the Proliferation of Weapons of Mass Destruction."

There are setbacks, which is not surprising given the mistrust that Iraq generates on both sides of the Atlantic. After the British accept a Franco-German proposal on 20 September for the EU to have autonomous military planning and operational capabilities, US NATO Ambassador, R. Nicholas Burns, warns that EU plans to set up an independent military headquarters are " . . . the most significant threat to NATO's future."[14] However, increasingly the institutional shape matters less than the need to generate real security in complex security environments. Some Europeans still hanker after a European defense without NATO and, by extension, American influence, some in the US and UK simply wish the ESDP would go away. However, slowly the utility of two security leadership hubs in the West starts to penetrate the political and institutional barriers of the preceding years. In the end, Iraq ends strategic pretense and paves the way for a new twenty-first-century transatlantic security relationship, founded upon the new world reality and a new transatlantic realism.

## European Security Strategy and Istanbul: Looking to the Future

When NATO was formed in 1949 Europeans had no option but to organize themselves *under* America. By 2003, the debate is about how to organize Europeans alongside America, particularly inside NATO. The facts are self-evident: the world is a dangerous place and getting more so; the transatlantic relationship is the cornerstone of both European and world security; there is only one set of Europeans, all of whom can afford at best limited armed forces. Whilst Europe and Europeans retain the right to determine their place in such a world, much of that action will necessarily take place alongside the United States. The extent to which the Alliance has gone full circle is demonstrated by two documents: the EU's December 2003 "European Security Strategy" (ESS) and NATO's June 2004 "Istanbul Declaration."

On 12–13 December, 2003, the Brussels European Council approves "A Secure Europe in a Better World – A European Security Strategy." It states that "Europe should be ready to share in the responsibility for global security and in building a better world … An active and capable European Union would make an impact on a global scale. In doing so, it would contribute to an effective multilateral system leading to a fairer, safer and more united world." The ESS goes on to identify five "key threats" which Europeans should engage; terrorism, proliferation of weapons of mass destruction, regional conflicts, state failure and organized crime. It also states, "The transatlantic relationship is irreplaceable. Acting together, the European Union and the United States can be a formidable force for good in the world. Our aim should be an effective and balanced partnership with the USA. This is an additional reason for the EU to build up its capabilities and increase its coherence."[15]

On 29 June, at NATO's Istanbul Summit, Alliance Heads of State and Government agree to expand the International Security Assistance Force (ISAF) in Afghanistan to include several additional provincial reconstruction teams (PRTs) and to conclude operations in Bosnia. They also agree to offer assistance to the Government of Iraq to train Iraqi security forces, and decide to enhance Operation Active Endeavour in the Mediterranean as part of the Alliance contribution to the Global War on Terror. Agreement is also reached to further transform the Alliance's military capabilities and it is announced that the robust NATO Response Force will reach initial operational capability in 2004.

Center-stage, however, are two initiatives that move the Alliance beyond its original purpose, whilst emphasizing the link with the Founding Fathers. The Istanbul Co-operation Initiative (ICI) aims to strengthen engagement with countries in the broader Middle East, through security sector reform and best practice advice on the democratic control of armed forces. In effect, the ICI looks to extend the security footprint of the Alliance beyond Europe by creating a new concept of partnership fundamental to its new strategic stabilization mission. The Alliance also launches "Our Security in a New Era" which re-defines NATO's mission in a new strategic age. The message is unequivocal: "Collective defense remains the core purpose of the Alliance. But the threats that NATO faces have changed substantially … NATO is transforming its military capabilities in order to adapt to the changing strategic environment. . . but transformation is a process, not an event."[16]

In these two documents are the foundations of the new strategic consensus, not just between Europeans and North Americans, but also between Europeans. It is not a foregone conclusion because Americans and Europeans today stand on the cusp of strategic convergence and divergence. But, given the strategic environment, only the most profound of miscalculations will prevent the West from doing what it has always done: aggregating democratic military power in the face of real danger. As Winston Churchill said, in a speech at London's Mansion House on 10 November 1942, on hearing of Montgomery's victory at El Alamein, "This is not the end. It is not even the beginning of the end. But it is, perhaps, the end of the beginning."[17] In other words, NATO is once again the focus for the systematic organization of the overwhelming power of the West in a new age. It is about doing what NATO has always done: adapting to change to best serve the security needs and interests of the pluralistic, democratic community of states that created it. It is about NATO today and NATO tomorrow, but it is also about the rediscovery of NATO's big security past.

On the morning of 11 March, 2003, commuters are jostling for space on several packed trains on their way to work in Madrid. In a few minutes 191 are dead. On the morning of the 7 July, 2005 commuters are jostling for space on several packed commuter trains and buses on their way to work to London. In a few minutes 56 are dead. It is a type of journey shared by millions of Europeans every day of their working lives. It is a type of death now shared by thousands of Americans and Europeans. It is a world gone mad . . .

# 2 Facing the Enemy

> The Parties agree that an armed attack against one or more of them in Europe or North America shall be considered an attack against them all, and consequently they agree that, if such an armed attack occurs, each of them, in exercise of the right of individual or collective self-defense recognized by Article 51 of the Charter of the United Nations, will assist the Party or Parties so attacked by taking forthwith, individually, and in concert with the other Parties, such action as is deemed necessary, including the use of armed force, to restore and maintain the security of the North Atlantic area.
>
> Article 5, the North Atlantic Treaty, Washington, 4 April 1949[1]

NATO has always been in crisis – and NATO has always endured. Indeed, it is the nature of the transatlantic security relationship to struggle and yet overcome. That is *the* lesson of the early years of the Cold War as the Alliance steeled itself for confrontation with Stalin's Soviet Union, and dealt with a range of internally and externally generated crises – the first Berlin crisis, the Korean War, German rearmament, the missile gap, the second Berlin crisis, the Cuban Missile

Crisis and the withdrawal of France from military NATO pushed the Alliance to the limit. However, NATO endured because no internal controversy was greater than the challenge posed by the security environment NATO had to confront.

## The Founding of an Alliance

On 4 April 1949, the North Atlantic Treaty is signed in Washington by Belgium, Canada, Denmark, France, Iceland, Italy, Luxembourg, the Netherlands, Norway, Portugal, the United Kingdom and the United States. Key dates in NATO's history are found in the timeline in the Appendix. As the clinking of champagne glasses in Washington fades, the situation the morning after is sobering. The Western Allies estimate that they can field some twelve active army divisions, whereas Soviet strength is estimated to be 175. If the Soviet Union is to headed off America must re-commit to Europe. NATO thus represents a revolutionary change in US foreign policy and the creation of America's most entangling of alliances.[2]

Events move fast. On 22 February 1946, American diplomat George Kennan writes a diplomatic dispatch that is to change US policy profoundly. The Long Telegram warns of the expansionist ambitions of the Soviet Union and that Moscow will use both overt and covert means to achieve a communist world.[3] Two weeks later Winston Churchill, in a landmark speech entitled the "Sinews of Peace," remarkable even by the oratorical standards of the great man, warns of an "Iron Curtain" descending upon Europe, from Stettin in the Baltic to Trieste in the Adriatic. Between 10 and 25 March 1947, US Secretary of State George Marshall visits Moscow and comes away firm in the belief that Kennan's warning is essentially correct. On 12 March 1947, President Harry S. Truman outlines what is to become known as the Truman Doctrine – the containment of Soviet expansionism. The Cold-War world takes shape.

The Cold War is essentially a conflict between two superpowers, America and Russia, driven by the extent to which they can promote their ideas and the manner by which they organize their partners. However, there are several sub-plots, particularly within the West, that help to give NATO's story a particular edge. At the center of US grand strategy is the re-birth of a democratic and economically vibrant Europe that will serve as a shining city on the hill in the clarion call to freedom. There will be times when Washington will wonder whether quite so much European freedom is a good thing, but it and they are measures by which the new "war" will be fought. To that end,

Washington calls on Western Europeans to specify their needs with respect to aid. The Marshall Plan is born, the greatest act of self-interested largesse in strategic history; and the most successful.

NATO has become synonymous with the confrontation between the two superpowers. However, in 1949 Europeans were as much preoccupied with the possibility of a resurgent Germany as an aggressive Soviet Union. Indeed, in February 1947 the UK signs the anti-German "Treaty of Dunkirk" with France, and in March 1948, the "Brussels Treaty of Economic, Social and Cultural Collaboration and Collective Self-Defense" is signed founding the Western Union, the first truly integrative European organization.[4] It is the first of many. The "German Question" is as yet unsolved for Europeans and causes particular consternation in a France already suspicious of the motives and intentions of "*les anglosaxons.*" The French newspaper, *Le Monde*, that 53 years later would trumpet Western solidarity the day after 9/11, suggests that the signing of the North Atlantic Treaty is a step on the road to West German rearmament to counter Soviet conventional strength. "The rearmament of Germany is present in the Atlantic Pact as the seed in the egg," the paper states.[5] Relations between Paris, London and Washington are already tense, not least because the US administration insists that France stop "dismantling" western Germany by way of war reparations and because of French demands for unity of command, i.e. a strong French voice in US policy. The tone of US–French relations is set.

By contrast, on 23 May 1949, West Germany is created. Western firmness pays off. The Soviets had agreed to lift the Berlin blockade some days earlier, recognizing that a policy of coercion has failed to force the Western Allies to retreat and adopt a more conciliatory tone. The tone of the Cold War is also established as Moscow adopts the mix of coercion and compromise that is to mark Soviet strategy.

On 25 July 1949, President Truman sends the Mutual Defense Assistance Act to Congress committing the US to foreign alliances even in peacetime. On 24 August 1949 the North Atlantic Treaty enters into force and the North Atlantic Treaty Organization (NATO) is born.

On 27 January 1950, President Truman approves an integrated defense plan for the North Atlantic area. On 1 April 1950, the newly-formed NATO Defense Committee approves the first draft of a four-year defense plan, "The Strategic Concept for the Defense of the North Atlantic Area," which sets out the strategy for territorial defense. At the same time, National Security Council Document 68 (NSC-68), outlining the overarching Americans' security policy and entitled "United States Objectives and Programs for National Security," is presented to President Truman, proposing a strategy of comprehensive Western rearmament even though Britain and France are against the rearming of Germany. As NATO comes into being so too are the seeds of NATO's first internal crisis. Indeed, whilst for Americans the Cold War is ultimately ideological, for Europeans it is profoundly classical. The Americans are confronting Soviet communism, Europeans are confronting Russians . . . and Germans.

But the need for cohesion is pressing. Much to the shock of the West, on 30 July 1949 the Soviet Union explodes its first atomic device. The Cold War has gone truly nuclear as the American nuclear monopoly is broken.

## The German Question

Nor is NATO the only show in town. Indeed, the early years of the Cold War also establish the rules of engagement for transatlantic relations evident today. The age of true European integration is about to begin and with it an argument over sovereignty and primacy that also continues to this day. It is a balance of power sub-plot that runs throughout the Cold War. On 21 March 1950, West German Chancellor, Konrad Adenauer, suggests an economic union between France and Germany to alleviate French fears of German intentions. On 16 April 1950, the so-called Schuman Plan (after Robert Schuman, the French Foreign Minister of the day) proposes the creation of a European Coal and Steel Community (ECSC) and eventually a federation of Western European states, focused on the Western European Union. On 9 May 1950, the French Cabinet approves the Schuman Plan stating that "World peace cannot be safeguarded without the making of a constructive effort proportionate to the dangers which threaten it. The contribution which an organized and living Europe can bring to civilization is indispensable to the maintenance of peaceful relations."[6]

However, in 1950 the strategic balance is still far too delicate for matters European to take center-stage – that must wait until the 1990s, although not for the last time it is disagreement over strategy that acts as a catalyst for European integration. On 25 June 1950 North Korea invades the south. The Korean War begins. The United States regards the invasion as yet more evidence of a Soviet-backed plan to expand communism globally and want Europeans to act in solidarity alongside them and hint at the possibility of re-arming West Germany. Europeans are not so sure. On 22 July 1950, the US High Commissioner in Germany states " . . . it is very difficult to deny the Germans the right and the means to defend their own soil."[7] However, the British and French

Governments reaffirm their opposition to West German rearmament, even though UK War Minister, Emmanuel Shinwell, confirms Western intelligence assessments that the Red Army has some 175 active divisions. Something must be done. On 11 August, Churchill suggests the creation of a European Army, whilst the Strasbourg Resolution of the Council of Europe calls for " . . . the creation, for a common defense of Europe, of a European Army under political institutions of a united Europe."[8] On 29 August, Chancellor Adenauer secretly offers West German participation in the defense of Western Europe.

Furthermore, on 9 September 1950, President Truman proposes an integrated military command to form the military heart of NATO. Truman also proposes a West German contribution of ten divisions. Not surprisingly, the French reject the proposal out of hand. One day later American forces land at Inchon on the Korean peninsula, increasing the pressure on Europeans to find more available military manpower. Moreover, on 16 September, at the North Atlantic Council (NAC) meeting in New York, NATO's senior political body, Alliance members agree to place the defensive line as far east in Germany as possible, increasing the need for West Germans to contribute. The Forward Strategy is agreed, as is the integrated command structure. However, France still refuses to shift over any West German military contribution.

Consequently, on 14 October, France proposes an alternative plan to rearm Germany, but outside NATO. It is the start of the Europeanist/ Atlanticist divide. The Pleven Plan, named after the French Prime Minister of the day, proposes an integrated European Army on the condition that Germany is only able to rearm as part of a supranational high command. On 28 October 1950, France introduces the Pleven Plan to the Allies at a meeting of the NATO Defense Committee.

This time America is not so sure. On 13 November 1950, the US reacts to the Pleven Plan with the Spofford Proposals for a German NATO contribution not to exceed 20 percent of overall force levels. Although Washington welcomes the creation of a European Army, as a means of strengthening the Atlantic Alliance, it does so only if it is militarily viable and operates within NATO. France remains implacably opposed to the Spofford Proposals because they imply German membership of the Alliance. But, not for the last time, an external event changes the dynamic within the Alliance.

In November 1950, Chinese forces cross the Yalu River into Korea. NATO must face a new reality and France backs down. Consequently, on 18 December, in a markedly changed strategic situation, the NATO Defense Committee approves the Spofford Proposals and on

19 December, General Dwight D. Eisenhower, the hero of D-Day, becomes NATO's first Supreme Allied Commander, Europe (SACEUR). Moreover, it is also agreed that West Germany shall have equality of rights and treatment. The modern NATO takes shape.

## The Rise and Fall of the European Defense Community

France's reputation for doggedness is not however without foundation. On 9 January 1951, the Petersberg Conference convenes outside Bonn to discuss a West German contribution to the defense of Western Europe. On 12 February, British Prime Minister Clement Attlee raises several conditions for West German rearmament, including the rearmament of NATO to precede that of Germany and for the West German contribution to be wholly integrated into a European Army. However, whilst the Paris Conference for the Creation of a European Army commences on 15 February 1951, with five participants, France, Germany, Italy, Belgium and Luxembourg, Britain is only an observer.[9] Having called for a European Army, Britain steps aside. It is to prove a watershed moment.

In parallel, on 18 April 1952, Belgium, France, Germany, Italy, Luxembourg and the Netherlands sign the treaty establishing the European Coal and Steel Community (ECSC). It is the first formal step on the road to the European Union.

It is not all plain sailing. On 4 June the Petersberg Conference collapses due to West German insistence on equality of treatment and France's determination to prevent it. And, in what becomes known as the change of heart, on 3 July 1951, Eisenhower calls for a European Federation and lends his support to proposals for a European Army and, on 30 July, formally authorizes US backing for the new European Defense Community (EDC). And so starts America's positive, but often confused, support for European integration. In return, discussions center on transforming West Germany's status from an occupied power to that of an ally. France adopts a position that sets a precedent – vetoing any such development within the Alliance, but offering agreement if it ties West Germany into European integration.

Furthemore, on 9 October 1951, a protocol is concluded inviting Greece and Turkey to become NATO members, marking the start of NATO's role as a container of conflict between members, since the state of relations between Athens and Ankara is poor. The US is concerned both are vulnerable to communist agitation. NATO enlargement begins as the Alliance's security footprint extends across the Old Continent.

By the end of the year the EDC is in trouble. It is the start of a complex relationship between London and Paris over Europe that will spill over into NATO, and indeed Europe, on many occasions. France says the EDC will fail unless the British join because they alone will be unable to counter-balance West German military power. Britain disagrees. Moreover, on 3 February, Chancellor Adenauer suggests that West Germany might only join the EDC if NATO membership is also offered. The US and UK, therefore, offer to support the EDC (although short of British membership) and to play their full role in the defense of Europe, by establishing a firm relationship between the EDC and the Alliance. It is the start of the protracted NATO/European defense debate.

On 14 March, the Paris Conference asks the UK to enter into a formal treaty relationship with the EDC. In response, Foreign Secretary Anthony Eden proposes the Eden Plan, whereby the Council of Europe would exercise political control over the EDC, i.e. an inter-governmental, not a supranational body, as envisaged for the EDC. And, on 9 May 1952, the "Traité Instituant la Communauté Européenne de Défense" is initialled in Paris with France still uncertain as to its commitments in the absence of an unequivocal British statement of support, even though renowned British Field Marshal Alexander visits Paris on 12 May to assure the French of a close British military association with the EDC. On 15 December 1952, Adenauer goes as far as to suggest a common foreign policy, saying that it is not possible to have a common defense policy without one. The seeds of a future debate are sown.

The EDC end-game has begun. On 4 November 1952, Dwight D. Eisenhower is elected President of the United States and on 8 January 1953, René Mayer becomes French Prime Minister and immediately demands more guarantees from the US and UK before France will ratify the EDC treaty. On 31 January, the new US Secretary of State, John Foster Dulles, embarks on a tour of Western European capitals to push for the EDC Treaty. Dulles is clear. NATO suffers from a "fatal weakness" without West Germany and the EDC. However, there is one other voice that must be reckoned with. Charles de Gaulle, France's hero of World War Two, bitterly attacks the EDC. Dulles responds by threatening aid cuts if the treaty is not ratified by 1 April. It is not. French Gaullism and Anglo-Saxon pragmatism are set on a collision course within the Alliance. It will not be the last time. Churchill responds by attacking France for its "anti-British" position and makes it clear the UK will not join the EDC. "We are with them," he states, " . . . but not of them."[10] The EDC is doomed.

On 29 October, the French Parliament formally calls on the UK to balance German power within the EDC. However, at the Bermuda Conference the British warn that if the EDC fails then preparations must begin for West Germany to join NATO. For the time being Eisenhower remains committed to the EDC and, on 14 December, Dulles warns of an "agonizing reappraisal" of US policy towards Western Europe if the EDC treaty is not ratified. The Secretary of State states unequivocally, it is EDC or nothing. But it is too late.

Although the UK signs an "Agreement Regarding Co-operation Between the UK and EDC," on 13 April, as the appointment of long-time EDC opponent, Pierre Mendés-France, as French Prime Minister, effectively ends any hope that France will ratify the EDC. On 30 August, the French Parliament adjourns discussion of the EDC treaty *sine die*. The European Defense Community is effectively dead and with it Europe's first great experiment in European Defense Union (EDU). It would be another thirty years before a truly autonomous European defense is re-addressed again. However, the primacy of the Alliance is established, and the way open for West German membership of the alliance.

The British move quickly to resolve the impasse. At the London Conference between 28 September and 2 October 1954, it is agreed to terminate the occupation regime in West Germany, to invite Bonn and Rome to accede to the Brussels Treaty, to allow limited West German rearmament, and, finally, to invite West Germany to join NATO. In return the UK commits itself to a permanent presence on the continent. It is the first time since the sixteenth century.

On 23 October 1954, the four treaties implementing the so-called "EDC alternative" are signed in Paris. The Western Union becomes the Western European Union (WEU) and is expanded as part of the amended Brussels Treaty. A Franco-German treaty foresees a European status for the disputed Saar/Sarre region, subject to a plebiscite (which subsequently votes for re-integration into West Germany). And, West Germany is invited to join NATO. On 24 October, West Germany formally joins the Alliance.

On 5 May 1955, the Soviet Union creates the Warsaw Treaty Organization (WTO) as a counter-balance to NATO. Lord Bruce Ismay, the first NATO Secretary-General, is reported as having said in 1952 that the purpose of NATO is " . . . to keep the Russians out, the Americans in and the Germans down."[11] The shape of Europe is set for the next thirty-five years.

## The Changing Nature of Nuclear Deterrence

Much of the inner-NATO debate is increasingly focused on the balance between nuclear and conventional forces. By the early 1950s there are three nuclear powers, the US, the USSR, and the United Kingdom. However, on 12 August 1953, the Soviet Union explodes its first hydrogen bomb, many times more powerful than the smaller atomic bombs. The nuclear arms race is well and truly under way. As the Soviet nuclear capability grows, so do American concerns for American vulnerability.

A conventional arms race is also underway. On 20–25 February 1952, the North Atlantic Council agrees the "Lisbon Force Goals," by which the Alliance establishes a force target of ninety-six military divisions by 1958. Not for the last time in NATO's history the Europeans pretend to get serious about enhancing military capabilities, and the Americans pretend to believe them. In time the failure to meet commitments generates major tension between the US and the Allies as so called burden-sharing comes to dominate much of Alliance politics. Indeed, as early as the North Atlantic Council meeting of 14–16 December 1954, and in spite of the Allies spending three and a half times more per year on defense in real terms than in 1949, it is evident that the Lisbon Force Goals are unattainable. European uncertainty over conventional capabilities is not simply a question of money. Many of them want the US nuclear umbrella to remain at the core of Alliance policy and paradoxically the European inability to close the conventional gap with the Soviet Union achieves just that.

Equally, the first cracks in Alliance nuclear solidarity appear. The development of tactical nuclear weapons represents a shift in US nuclear strategy towards a possible warfighting role on the European battlefield. As early as October 1951, the US carries out its first test of so-called "baby bombs," as part of the development of tactical nuclear weapons, and by 15 September 1953, the US reveals that it is deploying nuclear-capable 280mm cannon to Europe. In effect, American nuclear policy is becoming multi-layered, driven by strategy, technology and politics over which the European Allies have little control or say.

On 30 October 1953, President Eisenhower approves a new national security doctrine, NSC-162/2, entitled "The New Look," which advocates extensive reliance on nuclear weapons and strategic air power to deter communist expansion and aggression. Consequently, Eisenhower authorizes the expansion of the US nuclear arsenal and lays the foundations for what will become known as the doctrine of Massive Retaliation. That same month NATO formally adopts NSC-162/2 and becomes a true nuclear alliance, with first use by the West of nuclear weapons enshrined at its core. This might seem shocking today, but with the Alliance convinced of the superiority of the Warsaw Pact conventional forces, such a posture is the cornerstone of deterrence.

Still, Europeans are not so sure and Massive Retaliation marks the start of sustained European efforts to influence the use of weapons based on their soil that would not only run into the 1980s, but gradually erode American leadership over the Alliance.

Even though by the end of 1953 the Allies' defense spending is some 13 percent higher per year than in 1952, the North Atlantic Council of 14–16 December 1953 finally gives up on achieving the Lisbon Force Goals. The Alliance now moves into the politics of deterrence. The Europeans are not at all convinced when President Eisenhower suggests that nuclear weapons have achieved "conventional status." The Europeans *need* the US strategic deterrent to deter the Soviet Union, but they are concerned that a sub-strategic deterrent could lead to the de-coupling of America's nuclear guarantee from European defense in the event that deterrence fails. A concern that is to be further strengthened some two years later when in July 1956 news leaks that the US is planning to cut 800,000 personnel from the US Army, causing great concern in West Germany, which has only recently agreed to raise an army of 500,000.

However, Europe is but one theatre in the now global Cold War. On 13 March 1954, the French garrison at Dien Bien Phu in French Indo-China is attacked by communist insurgents, and falls on 7 May. At the subsequent Geneva Conference on Indo-China and Korea, France agrees to withdraw and the US offers to guarantee security in the region through a new regional security organization, the South East Asia Treaty Organization (SEATO). The Cold War continues its march beyond Europe as each of the superpowers seeks to outflank the other, and a new word enters the lexicon of danger – Vietnam.

### Idealism versus Imperialism

Dien Bien Phu marks another division within the Alliance – American idealism versus European imperialism. Indeed, American pressure to de-colonize is fueling the expansion of the Cold War as idealism replaces imperialism in many of the former European colonies. Or, to be exact, the Soviets attempt to insert communism into the former imperial possessions. Two events prove pivotal – Algeria and Suez. Since November 1954 France had been embroiled in Algeria, as separatists seek independence. By late 1955 some 517,000 French troops have been removed from NATO command to fight the insurgency. Such demands on French forces increase the strain on the Alliance as relations between East and West deteriorate. On 28–29 June 1956 a revolt by Polish workers is ruthlessly crushed by Soviet troops, whilst on 23 October 1956, Hungary revolts and Moscow moves rapidly to crush the rebellion.

Despite calls for Western help there is little the Alliance can do, embroiled, as it is, in its own crisis. On 26 July 1956, President Nasser of Egypt "renationalizes" the Suez Canal, depriving the British and French of a vital strategic artery to what remains of their respective empires. On 31 October 1956, with British and French collusion, Israel attacks Egypt. Under the pretext of separating Israeli and Egyptian forces, Britain and France invade. The US, about to face a presidential election, is appalled. It is blatant imperialism. In parallel, at the North Atlantic Council meeting of 13–14 December, the European allies demand access to US nuclear weapons stationed on their territory. The Alliance is in crisis. By 22 December, France and the UK are forced by Washington to withdraw. However, the Suez Crisis has three rapid consequences. The British Prime Minister Anthony Eden resigns, the end of the European Imperial Age is accelerated and France becomes more determined than ever to end its reliance upon the US. On 19 December 1956, France makes public its determination to develop an independent nuclear capability. Whilst France vows never again to be humiliated by the US, London takes the opposite view, effectively handing over British grand strategy to the US. However, security sovereignty is expensive for post-colonial European powers. Paris must leverage its power and that, in turn, means Europe must be molded as an extension of French power. A dividing line is established that endures to this day. On 25 March 1957, the Treaty Establishing the European Economic Community (EEC) is signed in Rome, by Belgium, France, West Germany, Italy, Luxembourg and the Netherlands. The Treaty declares that its aim it to " . . . lay the foundations for an ever closer union among the people of Europe."[12] Suez is a tipping point, both for the Alliance and Europe. German Chancellor Konrad Adenaeur happens to be sitting in the office of France Foreign Minister, Christian Pineau when Eden calls telling the latter that Britain is to withdraw from Suez. Adenauer's responsce is clear and compelling. "Europe will be your revenge."

## Berlin and NATO's Nuclear Dilemma

On 4 October 1957, another tipping point is reached. The Soviet Union successfully launches a satellite into space demonstrating that it possesses intercontinental ballistic missiles (ICBM) technology. If the Cold War hitherto had been Euro-centric, with that one act it goes intercontinental. American invulnerability is at an end. The Cold War is about to change and NATO faces a nuclear dilemma.

Not surprisingly the repercussions are swift. President Eisenhower meets with British Prime Minister Harold Macmillan to discuss providing the British with the technology to develop an independent UK deterrent.[13] Long in pursuit of its own capability, London is concerned that nuclear parity between the superpowers will undermine America's nuclear guarantee and yet is worried about the cost of its own nuclear program. The British are themselves prone to a bit of de-coupling. In May 1957 the UK announces the end of conscription and thereafter informs NATO that the British Army of the Rhine (BAOR) will be reduced from 77,000 to 55,000, just prior to the stationing of 60 US Thor intermediate nuclear missiles on British territory.

However, personalities also shape history and two very different men assume power who will have a profound impact on the Alliance. On 27 March 1958, Nikita Khrushchev becomes leader of the USSR. Even though he will pioneer the doctrine of peaceful co-existence with the West, he will also emphasize nuclear confrontation *with* the West. On 1 June 1958, Charles de Gaulle becomes President of France and a new era of confrontation begins *within* the West.

De Gaulle wastes no time. On 17 September, in a bid to break the Anglo-Saxon domination of the Alliance, he proposes a Triple Entente between Britain, France and the US. The offer is rejected out of hand, which consolidates de Gaulle's anti-British and anti-US position.

However, de Gaulle's *démarche* is soon eclipsed by a much more pressing issue – the status of Berlin. The city has long been a source of tension between the Soviet Union and the West, sitting, as it does, deep within the German Democratic Republic (GDR) or East Germany. On 10 November 1958, in a speech in Moscow, Khrushchev asserts that the Western powers have long since lost all legal rights to remain in Berlin and broken all agreements over a demilitarized Germany. He declares that the Berlin situation must be "normalized" and that Western powers leave Berlin. Ten years on from the first Berlin crisis, the second begins.

US Secretary of State Dulles declares that Berlin must be held and by military force if needs be. Moscow issues a double ultimatum: Western Allied troops are to withdraw from Berlin and Berlin must become a "free city". If not, then the USSR will sign a separate peace treaty with East Germany and transfer control of access routes between West Germany and West Berlin to the German Democratic Republic. The NATO Allies react swiftly. On 16–18 December 1958, the North Atlantic Council issues the Berlin Declaration which states the "Berlin question can only be settled in the framework of an agreement with the USSR on Germany as a whole."[14] The West is going to stay put.

However, 1959 does not start well for Alliance cohesion. On 8 January, Charles de Gaulle is inaugurated as the President of the Fifth Republic and in March, as the situation in Algeria worsens, he withdraws the French Mediterranean Fleet from NATO command. In June, de Gaulle attacks Alliance nuclear policy by stating that there can be no nuclear weapons on French soil that are not French, whilst in November he states that it is necessary that the defense of France be French and presents a plan to develop a French nuclear force, known as the *force de frappe*. Not for the last time, France triggers an internal Alliance crisis in the midst of an external crisis.

The strategic context is also changing. In December 1959, the USSR creates a Strategic Rocket Force (SRF) confirming, or at least appearing to confirm, that the United States is vulnerable to a Soviet nuclear strike. On 1 May 1960, Colonel Gary Powers is shot down by a Soviet ground-to-air missile in his U2 spy plane on a reconnaissance mission high over Russia. Shortly thereafter Khrushchev walks out of the Four Power Talks in Geneva. The Berlin Crisis deepens. On 8 November 1960, John F. Kennedy is elected President, with his promise to close the so-called "missile gap" with the Soviet Union.[15] As tensions develop the American nuclear strategy begins to shift. That same month, NATO SACEUR Norstad tells the NATO Parliament that the threshold for the use of nuclear weapons must be necessarily high. It is a clear move away from Massive Retaliation. The shift is due partly to US concerns for their own security, but also reflects Western European fears over tactical nuclear weapons in Europe, twin concerns that will remain central to the Alliance for the next twenty-five years. It is a seismic shift.

The results is NATO's nuclear dilemma: how to balance American control of nuclear forces, the emergence of British and French systems (the French test their first atomic device in February 1960) and a European desire for some control over nuclear weapons on their soil. In August 1960, State Department official Robert Bowie suggests that a multinational submarine missile force be established under joint command, with common funding and joint crews. Consequently, the Multilateral Force (MLF) is formally proposed to the Allies by the US at the North Atlantic Council in December 1960.

Furthermore, the new Secretary of State, Dean Rusk, suggests in a report entitled "A Review of North Atlantic Problems for the Future" that US strategic doctrine should move towards a much more flexible, graduated response to a Soviet conventional invasion of Western Europe that does not involve the early and overwhelming use of nuclear weapons. Consequently, Kennedy in a speech to the NATO Military Committee in April 1961 suggests that significant improvements are needed to Alliance conventional capabilities. Unfortunately, the NATO Allies see the speech as little more than a thinly disguised attempt to end the automatic use of the US strategic nuclear arsenal in their defense. To ease European fears of de-coupling Kennedy confirms the so-called "Polaris Offer" of five ballistic missile submarines to be placed under NATO control and calls for a NATO nuclear sea-borne force to be created, the Atlantic Nuclear Force (ANF).

On 6 February 1962, Chancellor Adenauer announces that West Germany is prepared to participate in the MLF, starting a long debate over the role of nuclear weapons in European defense. France is in no doubt. Paris announces that France will proceed with the construction of land, sea and air-based nuclear systems. The timing is propitious. On 4–6 May, US Secretary of Defense Robert McNamara bluntly tells a meeting of NATO foreign and defense ministers that the US will no longer automatically respond with nuclear weapons to a Soviet invasion. He also demands that US control over all NATO planning and European conventional forces must be improved. It is not what the Europeans want to hear.

The uneasy backdrop to all this is the Berlin Crisis. Khrushchev and Kennedy meet in Vienna, but reach no solution. Indeed, the Soviet Premier again threatens a separate accommodation with East Germany. As the crisis deepens it also accelerates as 33,000 people flee to the Western sectors of Berlin. On 25 July 1961, Kennedy warns that any attempt to block Western access to Berlin will mean war. The Soviets call his bluff. Between 13 and 16 August 1961, the Berlin Wall is constructed and Churchill's stark vision of an "iron curtain" descending across Europe becomes a concrete reality. Khrushchev convinces himself he can bluff the West into submission. The Cold War is about to enter its most dangerous moment.

## The Cuban Missile Crisis

On 14 October 1962, the US discovers extensive preparations under way in Cuba for the stationing of SS-3 and SS-4 intermediate-range ballistic missiles. It is the first direct superpower confrontation outside Europe and will lead to a new chapter in Moscow–Washington relations. The European Allies are mere bystanders, carried along in the wake of the superpower confrontation. For thirteen days the world teeters on the brink of nuclear holocaust, as Soviet merchant ships carrying missiles approach Cuba and the US prepares to stop them. Khrushchev blinks first and recalls the ships on 28 October. Quietly, the US signals it will remove Thor and Jupiter missile sites in Turkey and Italy. Armageddon is avoided...just.

The implications for inner-Alliance strategy are profound and well understood by the leading Europeans; and Americans. Kennedy quickly moves to offer Polaris to the British as part of an "independent" nuclear deterrent. It is the price the US must pay for Soviet nuclear parity. On 14 January 1963, President de Gaulle rejects the Polaris Offer, and in the same press conference rejects British membership of the European Economic Community (EEC).[16] Inner- and outer-Alliance politics merge. That same day, the Franco-German Elysée Treaty of Friendship is signed, which reconciles the two countries, and establishes a relationship central to European integration. Interestingly, the treaty provides for regular meetings between French and German ministers of defense, chiefs of staff and other relevant military authorities. The balance of politics within the West begins to shift, if not the balance of power.

Kennedy tries to repair the damage. In his State of the Union Address, one day later, Kennedy reiterates his vision for the Multilateral Force, claiming that the force would be a source of confidence, rather than contention. Were it so easy. In the months that follow the MLF proposal receives at best lukewarm support from the European Allies, demonstrating the almost schizophrenic nature of Alliance politics by the early 1960s. In June, as Kennedy tells Berliners, "Ich bin ein Berliner," France withdraws the French Atlantic Fleet from NATO. Sadly, on 22 November, President Kennedy is assassinated and Lyndon B. Johnson becomes President. Life is to get no easier for the Alliance.

## France's Withdrawal from Military NATO

Throughout 1964 the controversy over MLF resonates within the Alliance, with the British trying, as they so often do, to find a middle ground between France and the US and, as they so often do, failing. London proposes "mixed manning" whereby some nuclear weapons systems would be manned by personnel from across the NATO alliance. However, the real problem, as always, is political strategy. On 9 September, President de Gaulle drops a bombshell: France is to withdraw from military NATO. He cites French strategic independence and concerns over the faltering US commitment to the nuclear defense of Europe. De Gaulle orders all NATO forces and officials to leave France by 1 April 1966, and on 1 July 1966 French representatives step down from their positions in the integrated military structure. Cleverly, though, he does not withdraw France from political NATO.

Out of adversity comes opportunity. France's departure triggers a re-organization of the Alliance. On 26 October 1966, NATO establishes Brussels as its new headquarters and on 10 November, the Defense Planning Committee (DPC) requests that the Military Committee move from Washington to Brussels. A month later, on 14 December, a high-level Nuclear Planning Group (NPG) is created to give NATO members influence over Alliance nuclear policy and Belgian Foreign Minister, Pierre Harmel, who calls for a fundamental reappraisal of the political, military and economic aims of the Alliance, is charged with preparing a report to that end.

## The Strengthening and Weakening of the Alliance

1960s NATO is thus a strange combination of political and military strength and weakness. On the one hand, the deepening of the Alliance is apparent in the opening of SHAPE Headquarters at Mons in Belgium on 31 March 1967, and the first meeting of the Nuclear Planning Group in Washington. On the other hand, all NATO forces leave France and at the US–USSR Glassboro Summit, 23–25 June 1967, President Johnson tells Soviet Foreign Minister Gromyko that the US will enter talks on strategic arms control, effectively conceding parity to Moscow. Moreover, America's entrapment in Vietnam, and the nuclear stalemate with the USSR, is of concern to many Europeans as it appears that Alliance deterrence is failing, foreshadowing the Euromissile crisis of the 1970s. NATO is caught in the middle. On 29 March 1967, the first French nuclear ballistic missile submarine (SSBN), *Le Redoutable*, is launched. Whilst, on 2 October, the first British nuclear ballistic missile submarine (SSBN), HMS *Resolution,* joins the British fleet. It is no coincidence.

The period of strategic adjustment continues. On 13–14 December 1967, the North Atlantic Council formally adopts Flexible Response, a graduated response to a Soviet attack that, whilst it still enshrines nuclear weapons at the heart of NATO strategy and precludes the US from making any "no-first-strike" agreement with the Soviet Union, implicit or otherwise, further weakens the transatlantic nuclear link.

Towards the end of the 1960s the Cold War enters a complicated and complex phase. US strategy becomes progressively double-edged, given the need to balance European concerns and develop a strategic relationship with Moscow, particularly as the situation in Vietnam deteriorates. This is something the Brezhnev regime in Moscow is only too happy to encourage as part of the proxy global war. America starts to lose its strategic way. However, Moscow also has its problems. An uprising by the Czechs under their charismatic Communist Party leader, Alexander Dubček, is crushed when the Soviets and their proxies invade in August, demonstrating again the brutality of Soviet rule, particularly when Moscow enunciates the Brezhnev Doctrine whereby a move towards capitalism in one socialist country is seen to be a threat to them all.

NATO, as ever, reflects the transatlantic balancing act and the many strategic contradictions of the Cold War. On 24–25 June 1968, the North Atlantic Council publishes a declaration calling for mutually balanced force reductions (MBFRs) of conventional forces, in parallel with strategic nuclear arms control talks. On 1 July 1968, the Treaty on the Non-Proliferation of Nuclear Weapons is signed in Washington, London and Moscow. A month later Moscow surpasses the US in the number of intercontinental ballistic missiles (ICBMs) deployed, although the detail is somewhat semantic, as both superpowers possess enough nuclear warheads to render life on the planet extinct several times over.

On 5 November 1968, something else happens. Richard Millhouse Nixon is elected President of the United States. Nixon has very different priorities to Johnson, getting out of Vietnam being one. In effect, Nixon will abandon classical containment in favor of the search for a new global balance of power that also balances dialog with Moscow with confrontation. It is the start of the new American Realism, and with it détente. America starts to act in a very European way; and that really worries the Europeans.[17]

## Détente and De-coupling

As a consequence of the new American realism, European integration moves forward. On 3 October 1968, Pierre Harmel says that Belgium, the Netherlands and Luxembourg are to submit a plan to WEU for co-operation between the European Economic Community and the UK in the fields of foreign, defense, technological and monetary policy. The Harmel Plan suggests that the seven WEU members within NATO should establish a European pillar, and that European political co-operation on foreign policy, hitherto occasional, should become compulsory. On 13–14 November NATO agrees to the establishment of Eurogroup to better co-ordinate the defense activities of the European pillar.

On 1–2 December, the six EEC members agree to construct a European Community built on political, economic and monetary union and to open membership negotiations with the UK, Ireland, Denmark and Norway. On 27 October 1970, the foreign ministers of the "Six" formally endorse the "Report on the Problem of Political Unification," and with it what becomes known as European Political Co-operation (EPC). A Political Committee is established with a specific mandate to co-ordinate European foreign policies, in what will culminate with the EU's Common Foreign and Security Policy (CFSP) and European Security and Defense Policy (ESDP) in the 1990s.

Even as Europe attempts to organize a new strategic presence, it is being marginalized in American grand strategy. On 11 February 1969, Washington gives the go-ahead for the development of a new theater nuclear missile, which is detected by Soviet military intelligence and leads to the Soviet equivalent, the SS-20. On 25 July, the Nixon Doctrine is launched, by which the US adopts a classical carrots and sticks grand strategy to force the Soviet Union on the defensive, specifically by developing closer ties with a communist China, strengthening US military capabilities and trying to negotiate from strength with Moscow. To that end, in December, the US and Soviet Union agree to begin the Strategic Arms Limitations Talks (SALT) with the aim of stabilizing the strategic arms race. It is all above the heads of the fractious European Allies, as the new politics of détente and de-coupling come together.

In fact, the Allies have little choice; they can either support US policy or the US will act unilaterally. To assuage European concerns, on 12 September, the first nuclear-capable US F-111 bombers arrive in the UK, designed to penetrate Soviet air defenses. It backfires. Sensing an opportunity to split Americans from Europeans Moscow accelerates its plans to deploy a missile system designed specifically to strike Western Europe. Just as the strategic nuclear arms race slows, a new nuclear arms race begins in Europe with the Alliance firmly at its center. US grand strategy and European security seem at odds.

The double-edged nature of détente is apparent when, in December, NATO's AD-70 report suggests that Warsaw Pact forces have undergone significant modernization. In response, NATO's Eurogroup decides to embark on a package of force improvements in spite of the economic difficulties most are facing. The move is timely. On 13 February 1971, US Senator Mike Mansfield tables a motion calling upon the Nixon White House to withdraw 50 percent of US forces from Western Europe, if the NATO Allies do not do more for their own defense.

On 22–30 May 1972, Nixon visits Moscow to sign the SALT I and Anti-Ballistic Missile (ABM) treaties. SALT I fixes offensive nuclear capability at parity, whilst the ABM Treaty drastically limits the deployment of anti-missile systems, formalizing the mutual vulnerability that has been fact for a decade. On 29 May Brezhnev and Nixon also agree Six Basic Principles for Détente to underpin the co-existence of the capitalist and socialist systems. Europeans do not know whether to be relieved or appalled. There *are* benefits for Europe. On 3 June, a Four Power Agreement finally regularizes the status of West Berlin and paves the way for the normalization of relations between West and East Germany. It is no coincidence that as the SALT II talks start in Geneva in November, the Mutually Balanced Force Reduction talks start in Vienna. Whilst the former are devoted to further formalizing the superpower relationship, the latter concern the European–European relationship, specifically the balance between NATO and the Warsaw Pact. Strategic arms control is thus linked to regional arms balances.

Equally, ever more powerless, many Europeans believe it necessary to open up a separate strategic track. Consequently, the first summit of the enlarged EEC makes a clear statement about Europe's political ambition: "The member states of the Community, the driving wheels of European construction, declare their intention of converting their entire relationship into a European Union before the end of this decade."[18] It may not have seemed it at the time but the decision is a tipping point every bit as important as the Suez Crisis. The intent is clear: European institutional power must, in time, balance American and Soviet power.

It is an auspicious moment. On 21 December 1972, East and West Germany finally recognize each other's sovereignty. As superpower détente is established in the early seventies, so is a new Europe–Europe relationship, driven by West Germany's *Ostpolitik*, and opened up by a thawing in the Moscow–Washington relationship. It is a relationship between Europeans that will prove over time relentless and help eventually to create a Europe whole and free – NATO's abiding mission. And yet, the Alliance remains fractious. Indeed, détente merely provides the catalyst for the three great Alliance controversies of the 70s: de-coupling, burden-sharing and Euromissiles. It is going to be a bumpy ride.

# 3 Coping with the Allies

- The Forces of Divergence
- The Euro-strategic Balance
- The Second Cold War
- Reagan and Strategic Poker
- The Cold War End-Game
- Preparing for a Post-Cold War World
- The Crisis Management Alliance – Why NATO Won the Cold War

> . . . the thing that is troubling our European allies in particular . . . is not our military capability but what they perceive to be our shaky coherence and national unity which may make it impossible to use those military capabilities. It is the credibility of our commitment, not the existence of our commitments, or the strength of our forces that is the doubt in their minds.
>
> Amos Jordan, Principal Assistant Secretary of Defense for International Security, 1975[1]

As the US embarks on a new geo-political strategy, the balance of terror between Washington and Moscow shifts the focus firmly on to the Euro-strategic nuclear balance. European leaders oscillate between demanding more American missiles for their protection or insisting on less as Western European public opinion becomes increasingly nervous of nuclear war in Europe. Moreover, as Warsaw Pact forces modernize, the NATO Allies struggle to match them, crippled by the oil embargo imposed by Arab states after the 1973 Yom Kippur War. However, the Soviet Union faces its own economic problems as the burden of confronting the US and its Allies, and the suppressing of its satellites in Central and Eastern Europe, begins to demand a political flexibility that Moscow cannot offer. As the first stirrings of Islamic Fundamentalism begin to eat at its South, and democratic aspirations destabilize its West, the Soviet Union is forced on the defensive. In this time of fracture and uncertainly the Cold War moves forward its climax.

## The Forces of Divergence

The Alliance did not need the Yom Kippur War. On 6 October 1973, Arab forces cross the Suez Canal and attack Israeli forces, pitting a US client-state, Israel, against a raft of Soviet Arab client-states. As the attack falters the Arabs appeal for help to Moscow. For a brief moment it appears the war is moving forwards direct involvement of the superpowers. On 25 October, an under-pressure President Nixon orders US forces to a world-wide alert, but omits to inform the NATO Allies. Unfortunately, Yom Kippur triggers more than Alliance gripes over policy.

On 5 November, the Organization of Petroleum-Exporting Countries (OPEC) announces a 25 percent cut in oil production levels, leading to a doubling of the price of crude oil. European economies tip over into recession and the US and Europe begin a split over the Middle East that continues to this day. On 6 November, EEC foreign ministers not only "strongly urge" both sides in the conflict to return to the position they occupied on 22 October, but call upon Israel to end the occupation of territory it took in the 1967 war. This is directly counter to Washington's position and the US administration reacts with a veiled threat to withdraw from Europe.

Two other crises are brewing – Euromissiles and burden-sharing. Intra-Alliance relations were already tense. On 22 June 1973, the US and USSR had concluded an "Agreement on the Prevention of Nuclear War." The European Allies were deeply concerned that as the agreement precludes the use of nuclear weapons it negates a central feature of Alliance strategy. Indeed a group of visiting US senators was shocked at the level of European anger and warned Washington of the dangers to NATO if the US bargains without consulting the Allies.[2] On 6–7 November, NATO's Nuclear Planning Group establishes two committees, the Military Implications Team (MIT) and the Political Implications Team (PIT), charged with examining the likely impact of Cruise and Pershing 2 missile deployment on NATO strategy. On 7 December, in response to US complaints about burden-sharing, the Defense Planning Committee (DPC) looks to reduce US costs. The two initiatives could not have come at a more testing moment. On cue, nine EEC leaders agree " . . . to speak with one voice in important world affairs," as much to increase their influence on the US, as to deepen Europe's political identity. The need is pressing,[3] the question of nuclear weapons based in Europe in the defense of Europe comes front and center in the transatlantic relationship. Not surprisingly, Europeans are sensitive about nuclear war on their territory, particularly when the US again implies a warfighting role for nukes. On 10 January 1974, the Schlesinger Doctrine (NSDM 242) is enunciated stressing the use of low-yield nuclear warheads to strike Soviet military targets of opportunity to avoid what becomes euphemistically known as "collateral damage."

## The Eurostrategic Balance

It is in a testy atmosphere that, on 26 June 1974, the NATO Heads of State and Government sign a Declaration on Future Transatlantic Relations to mark the 25th anniversary of NATO. Less than a month later Turkey invades Cyprus and comes close to war with Greece. That is not all. On 8 August, President Nixon resigns rather than face impeachment for his role in the Watergate affair. Although Vice-President Gerald R. Ford takes up the reins of power, US leadership is badly weakened. Moreover, on 14 August, Greece withdraws from NATO's integrated command structure in protest at what it regards as the insufficient response of the Allies to the Turkish invasion of Cyprus. Shorn of a purposeful superpower, with two members on the brink of war, a new Euro-strategic balance emerges, changing the nature of the Cold War again and moving NATO back into crisis.

In November 1974, sensing an opportunity to split the Alliance, Moscow proceeds with the deployment of SS-20 missiles in Eastern Europe, and in so doing destabilizing the European nuclear balance as the missiles can strike forward American air bases almost without warning.[4] Moscow's political objective is clear; to force the Europeans to treat separately with them. Moreover, at a meeting of the North Atlantic Council on 12–13 December, whilst increases in Warsaw Pact forces are noted, the impact of OPEC-induced inflation on Allied defense expenditure is all too a apparent, in spite of a re-affirmation of the need to improve NATO forces. Indeed, even as Saigon falls to advancing North Vietnamese and Vietcong forces, the UK, the Netherlands, Belgium and Denmark announce unilateral defense cuts. To reiterate the point, at a ministerial meeting of the Defense Planning Committee on 23 May 1975, Eurogroup states that the effectiveness of the European pillar must be improved. A year later the European

Allies, under American pressure, agree to a year-on-year 3 percent increase in defense expenditure that few will honor. The gap between what Europeans need to do, and what they can afford, grows ever wider. It is a squaring of the European defense circle that continues to this day.

Unsure of American leadership, wary of Moscow's overtures, economically weak, militarily challenged, faced with the emergence of Eurocommunism in Western Europe and a modernizing Warsaw Pact, the Europeans are in a dilemma.[5] Their first instinct is to push for closer institutional ties. Indeed, it is the start of a trend that will see Europeans repeatedly re-organize institutions during times of crisis without ever really addressing the underlying absence of capabilities and resources. At an EEC meeting of Heads of State and Government in Paris new impetus is given to European integration to co-ordinate their diplomatic action in all areas of international affairs which affect the interests of the European Community. Equally, it is self-evident that Europeans cannot afford a European defense effort distinct from NATO if they are to maintain Eurostrategic balance. Consequently, even France begins to seek ways to co-operate with military NATO. The European Allies also seek alternative ways to improve their military capabilities through closer harmonization of their defense effort. If they cannot spend more, they can at least try to spend better.

On 2 February 1976, European NATO members agree to create an Independent European Program Group (IEPG) to better co-ordinate arms procurement. Equally, for the first time since 1966 France participates in a meeting of Eurogroup. Moreover, at a ministerial meeting of the Defense Planning Committee, amid concerns over Warsaw Pact modernization, the 1977–82 NATO Force Goals are endorsed. Three days later, the European Allies demand the US replace the aging Honest John and Jupiter missiles, with new Cruise and Pershing 2 intermediate-range theater nuclear missiles (INF) to restore the Eurostrategic balance.

The US is not deaf to European concerns. On 3 October, the US deploys a further 84 nuclear-capable F-111 bombers to Western Europe, and also initiates a study to replace the F-111s with Ground-Launched Cruise Missiles (GLCM). At the North Atlantic Council meeting in Brussels on 9–10 December, the Alliance totally rejects Moscow demands that NATO renounce the first use of nuclear weapons and limit the involvement of European states in alliances. Acquiescence would simply have confirmed both Soviet conventional and nuclear superiority in Europe.

However, transatlantic relations are not strong, and they are about to get a whole lot worse. As Jimmy Carter becomes American President in the fall of 1976, he orders Presidential Memorandum 10, a full review of the US force posture and structure in Western Europe. The Germans learn that as part of that review US forces would withdraw "temporarily" from the defense of German territory in the event of a Soviet invasion. They are not happy. On 21 March 1977, the Frankfurter *Allgemeine Zeitung*, with the alleged backing of the German Foreign Ministry, publishes an article which states: "Bonn is concerned that Jimmy Carter is a man ruling the White House whose moral and religious convictions are incompatible with the demands of world politics."[6] Not surprisingly, the relationship between Carter and German Chancellor Helmut Schmidt is difficult. The relationship deteriorates further as Carter and Schmidt confront each other over NATO's Long-Term Defense Program (LTDP).

To assuage European anger Carter orders Leslie Gelb, Director of the State Department's Bureau of Politico-Military Affairs, to prepare a report explaining to the Europeans the American technical and operational analysis of the European nuclear balance. Unfortunately, what the Gelb Paper reveals is a gulf in understanding between the Americans and European Allies over theater nuclear forces (TNF). Its main finding is that the deployment of cruise missiles would have the effect of de-coupling the US strategic arsenal from the defense of Europe precisely because it would create a Eurostrategic balance and thereby reduce the credibility of the US strategic deterrent. The European Allies, on the other hand, already believe that the US strategic deterrent has lost credibility and that a Eurostrategic balance already exists, particularly after the Carter administration publishes estimates of casualties in the event of nuclear war; 140 million in the US and 113 million in Europe. It is a long way from the 1950s.

Two events conspire to further complicate what is by now a full-blown Alliance crisis. First, at a meeting between the US Secretary of State, Cyrus Vance, and Soviet Foreign Minister Andrei Gromyko in Geneva, the Americans make a radical proposal: if the Soviets put a moratorium on the deployment of SS-20s, the US will delay the deployment of cruise missiles by three years. One minor problem: Washington again omits to consult the European Allies. Second, on 6 June 1977, the *Washington Post* reports that the US is seeking to construct an enhanced radiation weapon, or neutron bomb, designed to destroy concentrated Soviet tank columns through minimal blast to avoid collateral damage. The Soviet propaganda machine goes into overdrive and captures the imagination of a resurgent anti-nuclear movement in Western Europe.

NATO responds initially by appointing a High-Level Group (HLG) to examine outstanding strategic issues. However at the first meeting the Germans demand the Americans adjust their position in the SALT II talks to allow for the deployment of Cruise and Pershing 2 missiles. The US refuses. In a speech in London on 28 October, Helmut Schmidt says, "Strategic arms limitations confined to the US and the Soviet Union will inevitably impair the security of the West European members of the Alliance vis-à-vis Soviet military superiority in Europe if we do not succeed in removing the disparities of military power parallel to the SALT negotiations."[7] Crucially, the British agree with him. In December, the USSR begins deployment of the SS-20 and East–West relations turn decidedly chilly. West–West relations are not much better.

It is the Americans who give way. In January 1978, the NATO High-Level Group suggests an "evolutionary upward adjustment" in NATO Long-Range Theater Nuclear Forces (LRTNF) and on 7 April, the US abandons plans to deploy enhanced radiation weapons. On 20 August, *The Economist* states what is by now the obvious: "Some Europeans have always doubted whether the Americans would fight a nuclear war for Europe; and even the trusters are beginning to think that what might have been true when the United States had a commanding lead, is not necessarily true now."[8] In effect, NATO becomes locked in a struggle with the Soviets over the Eurostrategic balance for the hearts and minds of the very people it was created to defend. It is a struggle that will be the test of political strength for the remainder of the Cold War. In August, President Carter accepts an inter-agency report on LRTNF which supports the deployment of Cruise and Pershing 2 missiles. The Europeans have their way. Soon they will wish they had not.

In the midst of turmoil Alliance leaders meet in Guadeloupe. The US attempts to re-assert leadership within the Alliance by adopting a tough line. Ironically, it is now the Germans who are facing an embarrassing climb-down, as public opinion is strongly against the stationing of Euromissiles on German soil. National Security Advisor, Zbigniew Brzezinski, insists that the Germans accept the missiles even though there is little the Carter administration can do to force the Germans to change their new political position. Germany has come of political age.

Carter and Schmidt are not the only new political personalities changing the landscape of Alliance politics. On 3 May, one Margaret Thatcher is elected Prime Minister of Great Britain.

On 30–31 May, the North Atlantic Council meeting in Washington celebrates the thirtieth anniversary of the founding of the Alliance. The celebrations are muted. Although, on 18 June, the SALT II Treaty is signed, it is yet to be ratified by the US Congress or the Supreme Soviet. Moreover, in September, Henry Kissinger tells Western Europeans to stop being unrealistic about the use of the American strategic nuclear arsenal in their defense. It is not going to happen.

So, on 14 November, and in spite of Europe's political difficulties, the Nuclear Planning Group (NPG) agrees to deploy 464 Cruise and 108 Pershing 2 missiles in Europe by the end of 1983. All the Pershing 2s are to be deployed in West Germany, whilst of the 464 Cruise missiles, 160 are destined for the UK, 96 for Italy, and 48 each for Belgium and the Netherlands. The NPG also reaffirms the need for arms control to be pursued in parallel, reflective of a European demand that preparations for deployment take place in parallel with arms control negotiations. On 11–12 December, NATO's Defense Planning Committee adopts its five-year force plan for 1980–84 and at a special meeting of NATO foreign and defense ministers, it is agreed that unless the Soviet Union withdraws the SS-20 missiles the Alliance will go ahead with deployment of Cruise and Pershing 2 missiles by December 1983. The "Dual-Track" decision commits NATO to a program of deployment, but leaves open a negotiated settlement with the Soviets.

However, European governments are increasingly under pressure from public opinion. Consequentially, the Germans, Dutch and Belgians also insist that greater effort be made to achieve an arms control agreement with the Soviet Union covering Euromissiles, as their respective publics' opinion becomes ever more hostile to deployment. On 15 December, *The Economist* states that "In recent months, the growing Soviet nuclear superiority in Europe has posed NATO with one of its greatest challenges yet, both from the Russians and from those West Europeans who are reluctant to face up to the need to restore the balance."[9]

The only good news is that in September, Spain indicates a willingness to join NATO. One of the most ardent critics of Spain's decision is a Spanish socialist named Javier Solana Madariaga – a future NATO Secretary-General.

NATO's world is also beginning to move beyond Europe. On 16 January 1979, Shah Mohammed Reza Pahlevi is forced to leave Iran. Islamic fundamentalists seize power and America loses its main strategic partner in the Middle East. On 4 November, following

President Carter's decision to allow the former Shah into America for treatment, violent anti-American demonstrations in Tehran conclude with the storming of the US Embassy and the staff being taken hostage. Carter's greatest crisis begins. Moreover, on 27 December 1979, alarmed by the spread of Islamic fundamentalism in its volatile southern republics, the Soviet Union invades Afghanistan. The West reacts by accusing Moscow of blatant adventurism and aggression. The US sees the invasion as the end of détente, most Europeans disagree. The re-ordering of world order did not start with the fall of the Berlin Wall, but with the Islamic Revolution in Iran and the Soviet invasion of Afghanistan. The Second Cold War has begun.[10]

## The Second Cold War

On 3 January 1980, the US Congress suspends ratification of the SALT II Treaty as the Carter administration withdraws it. On 23 January, the Carter Doctrine is enunciated, committing the US to a new policy of containment, whilst reaffirming the aspiration for détente. The nine EEC foreign ministers attack the Soviet Union forcefully, calling the invasion a serious violation of the principles of international relations enshrined in the UN Charter. However, Americans and Europeans are deeply split over what action to take.

In April, the Belgian Government postpones again its announcement of its chosen base for Cruise missiles. In July–August, as the US boycotts the Moscow Olympics, all the Western Europeans participate. The sense of strategic divergence is reinforced when, on 25 July, President Carter issues Presidential Directive 59 (PD-59) ordering a major build-up in American military capabilities and the development of a rapid deployment force to intervene anywhere in the world. Seven years after the end of the Vietnam War the template for the contemporary American military is established. Inside the Alliance several European Allies are doing the precise opposite. For example, the Netherlands announces that it is no longer able to comply with the 1977 decision to increase defense expenditure by a year-on-year average of 3 percent. Military divergence begins that will last until the present. As the US re-equips and prepares for a new military age, most Europeans find the costs and burdens of security too hard to bear.[11]

Whilst the superpowers rattle swords over Afghanistan, four other events take place that are to mark NATO's future. On 4 May 1980, Yugoslav leader Marshal Josip Broz Tito dies in Belgrade and Yugoslavia starts its long, slow descent into anarchy and chaos. In August, a new trade union movement, Solidarnosc (Solidarity) is formed in Poland, under the leadership of a charismatic Gdansk shipyard worker, Lech Wałesa. That same month, Iraqi dictator Saddam Hussein invades Iran. Finally, on 4 November 1980, Ronald Reagan is elected President of the United States. The so-called New Right now controls both the White House and Downing Street. The Reagan–Thatcher years begin.

A split now emerges in Europe between the pro-American, Euro-skeptic Margaret Thatcher and most Continental Europeans, as the events of the 1980s, and Britain's perennially semi-detached status, spur "core" Europe to redouble its efforts to play a distinct role in the world. In January 1981, the German and Italian foreign ministers, Hans-Dietrich Genscher and Emilio Colombo, call for the strengthening of the political and security aspects of the EEC, as part of the Bonn–Rome Initiative. On 10 May, François Mitterrand is elected President of France and on 13 October the London Report on European Political Co-operation is issued, which proposes strengthening the role of the supranational European Commission in crisis management, broadening the EPC mechanism to include political aspects of security and for the first time reinforcing the co-ordination of member-state policies through a crisis management mechanism. To press home the advantage, between 6 and 12 November the German and Italian Governments write to all the other member-states to present a draft European Act that includes a declaration of economic integration and proposals for tighter co-ordination in the political, security and defense fields which, in 1982, transforms the European Economic Community (EEC) into the European Community (EC).

The Reagan administration has other matters on its mind – refocusing the struggle with Moscow on the strategic, rather than Euro-strategic levels, where American power is at its most effective. Washington wastes no time in challenging the Soviet Union . . . and offending most of the European Allies. Indeed, on 9 May 1982, US Secretary of State, Al Haig, a former NATO SACEUR, says the task ahead for this vital decade is the management of global Soviet power. On 19 October, President Reagan approves National Security Decision Directive 13 (NSDD-13) entitled "Nuclear Weapons Employment Policy," which envisions fighting and winning an extended nuclear war.

Europe is of a different mind. On 21 November, 400,000 people demonstrate against the deployment of Cruise/Pershing missiles in the streets of Amsterdam and the Dutch Government again postpones stationing the missiles on its soil, even though the Reagan administration begins negotiations in the Intermediate Nuclear Forces (INF) Talks with Moscow as part of the "Dual Track"strategy. In December, in a

Soviet-inspired attempt to fuel West German public opposition to Cruise and Pershing, Moscow permits discussions between the two Germanys over NATO's planned deployment. However, as so often with Soviet diplomacy, just at the moment when it makes headway, Soviets reveal their essential character. On 13 December 1981, under intense pressure from Moscow, Polish Communist leader General Wojciech Jaruzelski imposes martial law in response to a wave of strikes and civil unrest led by Solidarnosc. Moscow and its political creed are morally bankrupt, and seen to be so.

The pace of the second Cold War accelerates as it becomes clear it is moving towards an end-game. On 5 May 1982, NATO publishes an official document on force comparisons with the Warsaw Pact that paints the Western Alliance as being in an alarmingly weak and vulnerable position. It is time for a game of strategic poker.

## Reagan and Strategic Poker

On 20 May 1982, the Reagan administration issues US National Security Strategy (National Security Decision Directive 32), that confirms the US decision to break the nuclear stalemate of mutually assured destruction and, if necessary, fight and win a nuclear war. Most European Allies are appalled, especially as Soviet doctrine seems to be moving in a similar direction. In December, in National Security Decision Directive 75 (NSDD 75), President Reagan establishes three long-term objectives. First, containment of Soviet expansion and a moderation in Soviet behavior; second, encourage change in the Soviet system towards greater liberalism; and third, negotiate agreements that are in the interest of the United States. The Allies have little influence.

Reagan is, in effect, raising the stakes in a game of strategic poker with the Soviets under the rubric "Peace through Strength". Again, NATO and the European Allies are mere bystanders. In 1980 Reagan had said, "Let's not delude ourselves, the Soviet Union underlies all the unrest that is going on. If they weren't engaged in this game of dominoes, there wouldn't be any hot spots in the world." He later calls Soviets the "evil empire."[12] The days of peaceful co-existence seem a very long way off as the Cold War re-discovers its ideological teeth. Reagan ups the stakes even further when, on 23 March 1983, he announces his backing for an initiative that he believes will render intercontinental ballistic missiles obsolete through a futuristic missile shield, the Strategic Defense Initiative (SDI) or Star Wars.

Not for the first time most Europeans, with the notable exception of Margaret Thatcher, are profoundly uncomfortable. It is again no coincidence that at a meeting of the now ten EEC Member-States (Greece had joined in 1981), a Solemn Declaration on European Union is issued in which the resolve is to "create a united Europe, which is more than ever necessary in order to meet the dangers of the world situation, capable of assuming the responsibilities incumbent on it by virtue of its political role, its economic potential and its manifold links with other peoples." The statement goes on, " . . . convinced that, by speaking with a single voice in foreign policy, including political aspects of security, Europe can contribute to the preservation of peace."[13]

But the Soviets are not cracking just yet. On 28 June, new Soviet leader Yuri Andropov characterizes the current situation as being two diametrically opposite world outlooks, two political courses: socialism and imperialism. To make matters worse, in the midst of the war of words tragedy ensues. On 1 September 1983, a Korean Airlines Boeing 747, en route from Anchorage to Seoul, is shot down over a Soviet submarine base on Sakhalin Island; 269 people lose their lives, including a member of the US House of Representatives. The Soviets claim the plane was spying, the US that the plane was simply off-course. It is in fact the result of a series of errors and horrific lapses of judgment, but it could not have come at a worse moment. On 28 September, in response to US accusations, Soviet leader Yuri Andropov, who had become General-Secretary of the Communist Party of the Soviet Union (CPSU) following Brezhnev's death in November 1982, warns that American policy is on a militarist course. Some Europeans agree. He also reaffirms a Soviet commitment to "peaceful co-existence," even though, on 23 November, the Soviets walk out of the INF talks in Geneva and in December, 572 Cruise and 108 Pershing 2 missiles begin their deployment in Western Europe. However, whilst Belgium finally announces it will begin preparations to take Cruise and Pershing 2 missiles, the Netherlands again postpones the deployment until 1988.

As the Cold War moves towards its climax, so does the end-game of superpower overlay in Europe. The Alliance is moving towards another tipping point.

## The Cold War End-Game

On 23 January 1984, the White House sends a report to Congress accusing the Soviet Union of seven violations of the 1974 Anti-Ballistic Missile (ABM) Treaty, in an attempt to justify SDI, which itself is arguably in treaty breach. Impressed by US resolve, and in deep internal crisis, Moscow proposes talks on the prohibition of the militarization of outer space and a moratorium on the testing and deployment of space-based weapons. The reason for the crisis is clear. On 9 February, Yuri Andropov dies of kidney failure and is replaced by octogenarian Konstantin Chernenko, a temporary solution to the Soviet leadership crisis. A power struggle is getting under way in the Kremlin between conservatives and reformers.

Reagan seizes his opportunity. On 24 September, President Reagan, in an address to the UN General Assembly, states that "America has repaired its strength and we are ready for constructive negotiations with the Soviet Union." The statement offers a way forward. In October, the US suggests talks with Moscow covering arms limitations on all strategic offensive and defensive arms. On 6 November, President Reagan is returned with an overwhelming majority following the 1984 US elections, promising to continue his policy of "Peace through Strength." But eyes are not only on Washington. On 16 December, Mikhail Gorbachev, a 54-year-old senior Soviet party leader, visits the UK. Widely regarded as the next leader of the Soviet Union, he embarks on discussions with Margaret Thatcher, after which he receives unusual praise from the "Iron Lady," as a man with whom she can do business.

Change is also apparent in European defense. On 24 October, on the initiative of the French and Belgian Governments, a preliminary joint meeting of the foreign and defense ministers of Europe's moribund defense arm, the Western European Union (WEU), is held in Rome. The ministers agree to re-activate the WEU to strengthen Western Europe's ability to contribute to its own defense and to enable France to play a fuller and more integrated role. For many of the Europeans the re-activation of the WEU is also an attempt to pressure the US to consult them more fully. The Rome Declaration states the determination of ministers to " . . . hold comprehensive discussions and to seek to harmonise their views on specific aspects of conditions of security in Europe, particular defense questions; arms control and disarmament, the effects of developments in East–West relations on security in Europe; Europe's contribution to the Atlantic Alliance . . . and the development of European co-operation in the field of armaments."[14] The Rome Declaration is a first step to making the WEU the defense arm of the European Community. Indeed, Americans, Europeans and Soviets are already beginning to envision a very different Europe in a very different world.

Euromissiles remain pivotal. The Soviets insist that progress must be linked to the scrapping of SDI, and any agreement on theater nuclear forces must include British and French systems. Indeed, in January 1985, Soviet Foreign Minister Gromyko states that it would " . . . be unjustified if the North Atlantic Alliance obtained a kind of addition, a bonus . . . in the form of the British and French armaments. This is the crux of the disagreement in connection with the discussion of the medium-range weapons problem."[15]

However, although change is also imminent in the Kremlin, the new leadership is not above trying to split NATO, albeit with a more subtle approach than hitherto. On 10 March, Chernenko dies and is replaced, as expected, by Mikhail Gorbachev. On 12 March, the INF talks recommence after a break of fifteen months. At first, Gorbachev echoes Gromyko's warnings over British and French systems, but the West refuses to budge. In July, Moscow unilaterally suspends deployment of nuclear weapons in Europe. Importantly, on 2 July, Gromyko is relieved of responsibility for foreign affairs as Gorbachev strengthens his control over Soviet policy, and replaces him with Eduard Shevardnadze. That same month, talks are held in the Kremlin between British and Soviet parliamentarians, during which the Soviet Chairman suggests that to the extent that the EEC acts as a political whole, the Soviet Union is ready to seek a common language with it on concrete international questions. This represents a shift in Soviet thinking, treating Western Europe as a distinct political identity. This new thinking is reflected during a visit by Gorbachev to Paris during which he seeks to solve accumulated European and world problems. Vitally, he cites the economic imperative of the Soviet Union. In effect, Gorbachev is implicitly admitting that Moscow can no longer afford the Cold War.

A period of maneuvering ensues. On 3 October, Gorbachev offers direct talks with Britain and France over strategic issues, saying that Moscow cannot ignore British and French nuclear systems because of what the Soviets regard as their growing capability. On 19–21 November, Gorbachev and Reagan meet in Geneva, with the latter trying to convince Gorbachev of the mutual benefit of SDI, but fails; although both sides agree to accelerate progress towards a 50 percent cut in strategic weapons and on Long-Range Theater Nuclear Forces (LRTNF). Euromissiles are by now the key to ending the Cold War but no solution is in sight.

Gorbachev then ups the stakes. On 15 January 1986, he calls for the US and USSR to reduce by one half the nuclear weapons that can reach one another's territory, dependent upon the mutual renunciation of the development, testing and deployment of space strike weapons. Interestingly, Gorbachev also states that the first stage would include the adoption and implementation of a decision on the complete elimination of medium-range missiles in the European zone. Quietly, Gorbachev drops the demand that they receive "compensation" for British and French systems, merely suggesting that they pledge not to build up their respective nuclear arsenals. However, on 10 March, recently-appointed NATO Secretary-General Lord Carrington states that Britain and France cannot be expected to accept perpetual nuclear obsolescence.

Gorbachev is not deterred. On 26 March, he redefines the Soviet concept of security away from preparedness to take the offensive to one of defense sufficiency. Moreover, on 11–12 October, Reagan and Gorbachev meet in Reykjavik, Iceland. The Soviets surprise the US with a radical proposal to cut strategic weapons in the first five years of any agreement, and the remaining 50 percent over the following five years. Reagan initially responds favorably and agrees to apply this formula to all intercontinental weaponry. Gorbachev then suggests the complete elimination of US and Soviet Long-Range Theater Nuclear Force in Europe, excluding British and French systems. However, the talks fail when Gorbachev again demands scrapping SDI. A step too far for Reagan.

Nor are the Allies happy. At a NATO defense ministers' meeting in Scotland, the Allies again express concerns at the US negotiating over their heads. Their central concern is that whilst the US seems happy to negotiate away systems the Europeans see as vital to their security, they seem unwilling to discuss SDI. On 25 October, French Foreign Minister André Giraud states that the withdrawal of all American missiles from Europe would weaken the security of Europe, especially in view of other imbalances, particularly conventional weapons.

In 1987 events move rapidly as the Soviet economy begins to deteriorate. On 8 January, Gorbachev accepts failure in his attempts to link any arms control agreement to the abandoning of SDI and accepts that Euromissiles must be dealt with separately. On 3–4 March, the US delegation tables a draft agreement which the Soviets accept in principle, including intrusive on-site inspections which hitherto have been one of the major stumbling blocks. By early December all final issues of principle are agreed and, on 8 December, the Treaty between the United States and the Union of Soviet Socialist Republics on the Elimination of Their Intermediate and Shorter Range Missiles (the INF Treaty) is signed by Reagan and Gorbachev in Washington. Both parties agree to eliminate all their launchers and missiles within eighteen months of the ratification of the treaty. After some thirteen years the

Euromissile Crisis is over and with it, to all intents and purposes, is the Cold War.[16]

A few months prior, on 17 February 1986, the Single European Act had been signed in Luxembourg. The European Economic Community became the European Community (EC) and European Political Co-operation (EPC) was incorporated into the treaty, which called upon the signatories to formulate and implement a European foreign policy. For the first time security and defense are overtly included in a founding European Act. Even before the formal end of the Cold War the re-organization of the European West begins.

## Preparing for a Post-Cold War World

On 27 October 1987, the WEU Ministerial Council adopts a Platform on European Security Interests, following a December 1986 proposal by French Prime Minister Jacques Chirac. The Platform recognizes that, " . . . the constitution of an integrated Europe will remain incomplete as long as it does not include security and defense, [WEU foreign and defense ministers] intend therefore to develop a more cohesive European defense identity."[17] The Platform not only links the future of the WEU to the European Community for the first time, but also represents a clear statement of intent to develop a defense identity distinct to that of the Alliance. On 4 November, the Reagan administration, whilst welcoming the WEU Platform, hints at future discord, emphasizing the "unshakeable" nature of the United States' commitment to the Alliance and to European security. On 11 November, the North Atlantic Council issues a similar statement, welcoming the suggestion of increased European effort, but making it clear that such effort must take place within the Atlantic Alliance, affirming " . . . a positive identity in the field of European security within the framework of the Atlantic Alliance, conducive to the strengthening of the transatlantic partnership and of the Alliance as a whole."[18]

But INF has changed the rules of the West–West game. On 13 November, German Chancellor Helmut Kohl and French President François Mitterrand announce the setting up of a German–French Brigade. It is the first step on the path to the creation of Eurocorps. Furthermore, on 22 January 1988, a German–French Defense and Security Council is founded. On 19 April, the WEU Council even invokes the modified Brussels Treaty for the first time since 1955 following attacks on western oil tankers in open waters, mainly by Iran, leading to Operation Cleansweep, the first joint military operation conducted by the organization in its forty-year history.

Slowly at first, but with gathering vigor, Churchill's Iron Curtain is finally torn down. On 23 March, Gorbachev speaks of the need for more private initiative in Soviet agriculture. On 14 April, Afghanistan and Pakistan sign an agreement, with the US and USSR as guarantors, calling for the immediate withdrawal of Soviet military forces from Afghanistan. At a meeting on 23 May of the Hungarian Socialist Workers' Party it is agreed to separate the function of state and party – a major reform. On 29 June, at a press conference chaired by Gorbachev, Soviet politicians and economists demand major reforms to allow the process of democratization to proceed. On 3 July, the All-Union Congress of the CPSU endorses proposals for dramatic reforms of political institutions and, on 1 December, the Supreme Soviet approves the establishment of a new legislative body, the Congress of People's Deputies. NATO's great adversary begins to shrivel up without a struggle.

1989 breaks with a mood of universal anticipation. On 24 February, the Hungarian Socialist Workers' Party renounces its constitutionally based claim to leadership. On 26 March, for the first time Soviet citizens can choose from among several candidates in elections to the first Congress of Soviet People's Deputies. On 17 April, Solidarnosc is legalized in Poland and its representatives allowed to run for office.

On 5 June, elections in Poland result in a resounding victory for Solidarnosc, which inspires a series of by and large peaceful revolutions in Central and Eastern Europe, as country after country takes back sovereignty which many of them had lost in 1939 on the outbreak of World War Two. The sense of euphoria mounts by the day until, on 7 July, Soviet President Gorbachev concedes that every socialist state has the right to choose its own political path. The Brezhnev Doctrine is buried and replaced by the "Sinatra Doctrine," as each Central and Eastern European state is invited by Moscow to "do it their way." They do just that as an irresistible surge of people power casts the division of Europe into history.

On 19 August, some 900 East Germans flee over the so-called "green border" from Hungary to Austria, taking advantage of the "Pan-European Picnic" organized by the President of the Pan-European Union (and not without some historical irony) Otto von Hapsburg. On 23 August, tens of thousands of Balts form a human chain between the capitals of Estonia and Lithuania to protest against the Hitler–Stalin Pact of August 1939 which had deprived them of their liberty. The next day, the Hungarian Government permits 108 East German citizens to leave for the West and, on 4 September, the first of the mass Monday Demonstrations takes place in Leipzig, East

Germany, as people demand a whole raft of freedoms long denied them.

It is not all plain sailing. After some 7600 East German citizens are transported to the West from Czech territory on chartered trains on 30 September and 1 October, the East German Government closes the border with Czechoslovakia. It is too late. On 7 October, Gorbachev comes to East Berlin and lectures their leader, Erich Honecker, on the need for reform. As Moscow effectively abandons East Germany, 70,000 people demonstrate in Leipzig chanting, "We are the People." On 18 October, Honecker resigns to be replaced by Egon Kranz, but the Communist Party's control of the German Democratic Republic is fast collapsing. On 3 November, the East German Government permits its people to leave for the West via Czech territory. On 4 November, between five hundred thousand and one million people demonstrate in favor of democratic reform. East German television broadcasts the event live. On 7 November the East German Government steps down and on 9 November, the un-thinkable happens. Tens of thousands of people start converging on the Berlin Wall. Slowly at first, but with a steady increase in the tempo of their determination, that most potent of symbols of the Cold War is torn down slab by slab. At that moment there is neither West nor East Germany, just Germany. The German question is finally solved in favor of freedom.

They may not have known it but the people who dismantled the Berlin Wall are fulfilling slab by slab the aims of the North Atlantic Treaty scribed all those years before. They are making Europe whole and free. The Cold War is truly at an end as democracy ripples across a Europe becoming more whole and more free by the day. It is a stunning moment in history that could only have been dreamt of back in the nervous 1950s as NATO got to grips with the towering menace of the Red Army. NATO did nothing, but NATO meant everything. NATO won the Cold War.

## The Crisis Management Alliance – Why NATO Won the Cold War

NATO succeeded in the Cold War for three reasons. First, NATO proved itself a durable political as well as military mechanism serving the pluralistic community of democracies for which it was designed. The many arguments were in fact part of its strength. Second, over the length of the Cold War the Alliance developed an internal iden-tity; day after day, week after week, patient NATO civilians and military personnel established the largest body of international politico-military ties ever known. Third, the power of solidarity and the deterrent effect NATO generated proved decisive.

In a sense, NATO became the quintessential crisis management tool, even as it conducted collective defense. This is not so much crises between the superpowers which, after the Cuban missile crisis, they handled by and large directly, but rather crisis management between Alliance members. Indeed, the Alliance changed markedly between 1949 and 1989. In 1949 NATO was a mechanism for the organization of Europeans behind American leadership. By 1989 it had become the forum for the political conduct of the strategic transatlantic relationship. There were those Americans who continued to believe they could return to the "good old days" when the Soviet threat by and large organized Europeans on their behalf. Those days were long gone. Indeed, each major impulse towards European integration came at a time when America and the leading Europeans were in disagreement over strategy, or when America was perceived to be weak. The Korean War took place in parallel to the founding of the European Coal and Steel Community (ECSC). The creation of the European Economic Community (EEC) occurred as the Soviets began to develop their own advanced nuclear systems. Britain negotiated its membership of the EEC in the late 1960s at a time when the Special Relationship was in a particularly poor state. European Political Co-ordination happened against the backdrop of disarray in the second Nixon administration, the defeat in Vietnam and the shock of the Yom Kippur War. The re-activation of the WEU took place in the midst of the Euromissiles crisis. Put simply, a political balance of power was always implicit within the Alliance, and NATO acted as a mechanism for the governance of that balance. That is precisely why in 1966 the French left the integrated military command, i.e. military NATO, but did not leave political NATO. And so it continues.

The Warsaw Pact ultimately failed because it lacked the political vigor and rigor that only democracies can invest in alliances. Unable to challenge the Soviet Union directly, as so tragically demonstrated in Berlin in 1953, Hungary in 1956 and Prague in 1968, the Warsaw Pact simply became a mechanism of tutelage. For all America's many faults its central belief in the power of liberty was the winning idea that NATO embodied. Of course, the looming presence of the Soviet Union helped.

However, there was something more, something deeper, more profound than simply the balance of power that kept NATO together. The rest of the book explores just what that "something" was; and is.

# 4 Strategic Vacation

- NATO and the Re-ordering of Europe
- The First Gulf War
- NATO Security versus European Security
- NATO and the Echoes of the Past
- The Yugoslav Meltdown
- Enlargement and Divergence
- Strategy, History and Technology
- The Modernization of NATO
- The EU Alternative
- France's Near "Rapprochement" with NATO
- NATO and the Bosnian End-Game

> To protect peace and to prevent war or any kind of coercion, the Alliance will maintain for the foreseeable future an appropriate mix of nuclear and conventional forces based in Europe ... the overall size of the Allies' forces, and in many cases their readiness, will be reduced and the maintenance of a comprehensive in-place linear defensive posture in the central region will no longer be required ... Alliance forces will require enhanced flexibility and mobility and an assured capability for augmentation when necessary. For the Allies concerned, collective defense arrangements will rely increasingly on multinational forces, complementing national commitments to NATO.
>
> NATO's New Strategic Concept, November 1991[1]

For much of the 1990s NATO would be focused on four consequences of victory. First, re-assessing the value of American leadership; second, adjusting to collective security; third, considering the balance between effectiveness and legitimacy in promoting security; and, fourth, striking a balance between European aspirations and European capabilities. Indeed, the 1990s would be a security experiment for Europe. Indeed, as the Cold War ends the complexity of constructing the European political edifice leads to a form of European isolationism precisely because Europe becomes so focused on building its own shining city on the hill with its very regional sense of manifest destiny:[2] a work in progress that is still under way. NATO ceases to be the macro-defense shield of the West, and becomes instead the micro-manager of instability and insecurity across the Continent. To that end, NATO must both organize military cohesion, *and* incorporate political fragmentation, and all on a markedly reduced budget. Furthermore, there is also an underlying political dynamic as France, in particular, sees an opportunity finally to shape Europe, for the benefit of France. And of course, France and Germany seek to embed themselves firmly at the heart of the ideal of European political union. It is a *démarche* that will reinforce divide between the Europeanist and Atlanticist camps within the West and which shapes much of the debate today.

Nor is NATO invulnerable to change in the balance of power. Indeed, the Alliance will spend much of the 1990s trying to cope with a shift that would have destroyed most alliances in a previous age. Although, it is not only the shifting balance of political power in Europe that challenges the Alliance, so much as the rapidly widening gap between what American and European militaries can do and the impact of that gap on how the Allies see the role and the use of armed forces. It is a gap reinforced by the American desire to use great military power to avoid the nation-building, muddy boots facts of post-Cold War engagement, and a European tendency to take the end of history all too literally and become too focused on internal challenges.[3] In effect, much of European NATO goes on strategic vacation, whilst America starts to prepare for a new age of hyper-power. There are good reasons for Europe's relaxation. Whilst the US has been engaged in systemic conflict since 1941, the Europeans had been locked in a struggle, or coping with its consequences, since the Franco-Prussian War ended in 1871. It is time to recoup the costs of struggle. In short, victory in the Cold War imposes burdens and responsibilities on the victors that few are ready or willing to face. In such circumstances, squaring the new NATO circle proves no easy task.

## NATO and the Re-ordering of Europe

At the landmark London Summit of 5–6 July 1990, the North Atlantic Council begins the re-organization of NATO and its mission. NATO is to reduce its forward presence and nuclear weapons are deemed no longer weapons of first resort, but last. The great fifty-year nuclear debate is over – at least for the time being. The NATO Strategic Concept (the what, why, when, where and how of Alliance engagement) is also announced as an authoritative statement of NATO's grand strategic mission and lays out a broad approach to security in the post-Cold War world, encompassing complementary political and military means and emphasizing co-operation with other states that share the Alliance's objectives. NATO also makes a commitment to non-aggression with the Warsaw Pact members, confirming that the two organizations are no longer enemies, and invites Central and Eastern European leaders to address the Alliance. And, NATO leaders announce that the "Alliance will do its share to overcome the legacy of decades of suspicion," and that they are " . . . ready to intensify military contacts, including those of NATO Military Commanders, with Moscow and other Central and Eastern European capitals."[4] The long road to NATO enlargement is under way.

Interestingly, at the same meeting, President Mitterrand also announces that France will withdraw all troops from Germany by 1994, as do the Soviets. It is the inner-space of the new Alliance politics. France and Britain had been lukewarm about German re-unification and it is Chancellor Helmut Kohl, with American support, who drives the process forward. By July, both London and Paris have bowed to the inevitable, albeit not always with good grace, and begin jockeying for position with what would be Europe's largest most powerful economy – and least sure strategic actor. On 12 September, the Treaty on the Final Settlement with Respect to Germany (also known as the Two-Plus-Four Treaty) is signed by the Federal Republic of Germany, the German Democratic Republic, France, the Soviet Union, the UK and the US. For the first time since the end of World War Two, a united Germany is accorded a de facto peace treaty and full sovereign rights. Allied sovereign rights are to cease as of 3 October 1990. German re-unification takes place as seven newly created Länder, the German equivalent of states, accede to the Federal Republic of Germany. West and East Germany are officially no more.

The formal end of the Cold War takes place in Paris, as eras so often do. On 19 November 1990, the Conventional Armed Forces in Europe (CFE) Treaty is signed by twenty-two states representing NATO and the Warsaw Pact at the Conference on Security and Co-operation in Europe (CSCE). The treaty provides for equal ceilings for major weapons and equipment systems for both groups of states, which are then translated into national limits for each state. The participating states also sign the Charter of Paris for a New Europe establishing the permanent bodies of the CSCE, as NATO and the Warsaw Pact issue a statement that they are no longer enemies.

Not surprisingly, there are deep cuts in the Alliance defense effort. On 25 July 1990, UK Defense Secretary, Tom King, announces "Options for Change," cutting British military manpower by 18 percent and British forces in Germany by half to 30,000. All other European states follow, seduced by the opportunity of a defense premium. The Americans are not immune either to post-Cold War demobilization. In April, the US announces the Base Force Plan for the restructuring of US forces and their commands, but it is a relatively minor pruning compared with the European Allies. Indeed, in the 1990s cuts are often presented as modernization.

Mobility becomes the new buzzword. At a meeting of the NATO Defense Planning Committee (DPC) on 28–29 May 1991, NATO begins its adjustment away from main defense forces to rapid reaction and crisis management. The DPC announces the creation of a 30,000-strong Allied Command Europe Rapid Reaction Corps (ARRC) under British leadership, designed to respond to crises anywhere around Europe, reflecting both the need to cut forces and to pre-empt French attempts to make the European Community the focus of European crisis management. The creation of the ARRC also presages another debate that will rumble on throughout the 1990s – "out of NATO area." The need to engage crises not just in Europe, but beyond, as the burden of victory becomes apparent even in the early 1990s.

On 19 November, "A Transatlantic Declaration" heralds a new era in US–European relations.[5] In fact, whilst the Declaration is an overt statement of the enduring importance of the transatlantic relationship, there is an element of defensiveness therein that is to run through the 1990s. This is because the march of the European institutions begins as the European Community prepares to become the European Union.

## The First Gulf War

On 2 August 1990 Iraq invades Kuwait. On 17 January 1991, after months of military build-up and the ignoring by Iraq of UN demands for its withdrawal from Kuwait, a US-led coalition begins Operation Desert Storm. It is not a NATO operation, and the pointed avoidance of Alliance planning assets and capabilities by the US military is a sign of things to come, but in many ways Desert Storm is the large-scale, firepower and maneuver campaign for which the Alliance prepared over many years – against an enemy trained and equipped by the Soviet Union. So desperate are the Iraqis to escape the onslaught Saddam even sends his air force to seek refuge with his arch enemy Iran. On 24 February, the ground war, Operation Desert Saber, starts and by 26 February Iraqi forces start to withdraw from Kuwait promptly; and are massacred in the Mitla Gap by American and British air and tank power. Indeed, Allied strategy reflects the doctrine of Air Land Battle, first adopted by the US Army in 1982 (and also known as Follow-On Force Attack (FOFA)), that were at the heart of NATO's military strategy during the later years of the Cold War. Designed to counter Warsaw Pact numerical superiority, Air Land Battle attacks reserve forces to prevent them reinforcing an attack. Its emphasis is on choke points and killing zones, which are employed to terrifying effect on the "road of death" between Kuwait and Basra. It is a sobering example of what might have happened if the Group of Soviet Forces Germany (GSFG) had ever taken on NATO in the 1980s.

On 27 February it is all over. Kuwait is liberated and coalition forces cease hostilities. Although the performance of American personnel and equipment is hyped, with footage of cruise missiles going through windows to hit targets, the first Gulf War is a fitting accompaniment to NATO's European victory. The US is militarily supreme as it demonstrates American superiority in a classical military engagement. The Europeans do well, particularly the British, but they are by and large an adjunct. It is also a sign of the times to come.

On 3 April, the UN Security Council passes Resolution 687 demanding that Iraq unconditionally accept the destruction, removal or rendering harmless of all chemical and biological weapons. Resolution 687 also goes on to prohibit missiles with a range greater than 150 kms. To ensure compliance, the UN Security Council creates the UN Special Commission (UNSCOM) to carry out intrusive on-site inspections and mandates the International Atomic Energy Agency (IAEA) to verify Iraqi nuclear disarmament. At the moment of victory so the seeds of a future war are sown.

However, Saddam remains . . .

## NATO Security versus European Security

On 9–10 December 1991, the landmark Treaty on European Union (TEU) is approved at Maastricht. Title V of the Treaty contains "Provisions on a common foreign and security policy," with Article

J.4.1 stating as its goal, " . . . the implementation of a common foreign and security policy, including the eventual framing of a common defense policy, which might in time lead to a common defense."[6] On 10 December, Western European Union (WEU) is defined as the defense component of the European Union and a means to strengthen the European pillar of the Atlantic Alliance. For all the careful wording, the separate political tracks that started back in the 1950s with the European Defense Community (EDC) are now released from the shackles of Cold War and begin to diverge. Moreover, on 12 December, the Maastricht European Council agrees that the EU will take joint action over disarmament, arms control, nuclear non-proliferation and economic aspects of security, hitherto only the preserve of the super-powers. It is a sign of the changing strategic landscape.

Competition slowly emerges between the EC and NATO, often in the guise of strengthening the European pillar of the Alliance, but also reinforced by the belief of many Europeans that the new age is to be an age of "soft" security in which hard military instruments will be only of the most limited value. The Europeanist and Atlanticist camps become established around their respective champions, France and Germany on one side, the US and UK on the other. In February 1990, France and Germany had re-emphasized their commitment to a European Union, and on 14 October, Chancellor Kohl and President Mitterrand had proposed expanding the French–German Joint Brigade into " . . . the basis for a Eurocorps, to which the armed forces of other WEU member-states could be added."[7] The US has been wary of these developments for some time. At the North Atlantic Council meeting in Copenhagen on 6–7 June 1991, the US threatens to pull out of Europe, if the European Community takes responsibility for security matters. The battle lines of the 1990s are drawn.

But there is another Europe. At the same Copenhagen meeting the first tentative steps towards NATO enlargement are taken. Whilst NATO ministers refuse to give security guarantees to Central and Eastern European states they make it clear that European security is indivisible. On 7–8 November, at NATO's Rome Summit, the STOT Strategic Concept (NSC) is adopted, establishing the framework for the ARRC. The final communiqué represents an historic shift in the Alliance's mission as NATO evolves from an organization charged with the responsibility of protecting the territory of its members to assuring the security of the entire European space. Finally, the New Strategic Concept looks to the future, "For the Allies concerned, collective defense arrangements will rely increasingly on multinational forces, complementing national commitments to NATO."[8]

On 20 December, the North Atlantic Co-operation Council (NACC) is created as a consultative forum for NATO members and nine Central and Eastern European countries. This initially includes the Soviet Union, although at the closing session Moscow insists that all reference to the Soviet Union be deleted from the document. Also a sign of the times to come.

As Europe consolidates, the Soviet Union implodes. On 24 April 1991, Mikhail Gorbachev announces his resignation as General Secretary of the Communist Party of the Soviet Union, but it is rejected. On 12 June, Boris Yeltsin is elected President of the Russian Soviet Federal Socialist Republic (RSFSR), on 1 July, the Warsaw Pact is formally dissolved. Between 20 August and the end of December, Estonia, Latvia, Ukraine, Belarus, Moldova, Azerbaijan, Kyrgyzstan, Uzbekistan, Tajikistan, Armenia, Turkmenistan and Kazakhstan declare independence from the USSR. In spite of a desperate coup attempt by the Old Guard, the fate of the Soviet Union is sealed.

On 21 December, the Commonwealth of Independent States (CIS), set up as a successor grouping to the Soviet Union, confirms its formation of itself, and the USSR ceases to exist. On 24 December, Yeltsin informs the Secretary-General of the UN that the name "Russian Federation" should be used in the United Nations in place of the Union of Soviet Socialist Republics. The Soviet Union becomes a footnote in history. In its place the West must now deal with a humiliated, unstable nuclear Russia.

## NATO and the Echoes of the Past

Between 31 May and 3 June 1990, Washington and Moscow agree to recommence the Strategic Arms Limitation Reduction Talks (START) to reduce the risk of accidental launches. This includes the removal of warheads from all multi-tipped missiles (MIRVs). Once the neurotic, obsessive epicenter of the Cold War, by 1990 such weapons seem passé, although as the Soviet Union descends into oblivion secure control over its nuclear forces becomes a central issue for the Alliance. For example, in 1991 Kazakhstan becomes the world's newest and third largest nuclear power.

On 29 January, President Bush announces cuts in the Strategic Defense Initiative (SDI), although the search for American invulnerability continues. Always primarily a political initiative to break the back of the Soviet strategic effort, the US is in reality many years from ever achieving a functioning missile defense system. Officially, Global Protection Against Limited Strikes (GPALS) is designed to protect the

US from unauthorized, accidental attacks from Soviet warheads, although first mention is also made of attacks by so-called "rogue states," which will come to dominate US grand strategy in years to come. In effect, missile defense is put on hold, but never scrapped.

Consequently, on 31 July 1991 the START Treaty is signed, reducing the nuclear arsenals of America and Russia to a limit of 3500 warheads apiece. Interestingly, in so doing the relative importance of the modernizing British and French capabilities increases, the very thing that so worried Moscow back in the early 1980s.

## The Yugoslav Meltdown

If the Treaty on European Union marked the extent of European ambitions, the Wars of Yugoslav Succession establish their limits, and the continued reliance of the Old Continent upon the US and NATO for all but the most modest of security missions. Moreover, they also demonstrate that collective security is as devilishly difficult to maintain as it ever was, raising profound questions on both sides of the Atlantic about the respective roles of Americans and Europeans in the post-Cold War world and, in particular, NATO and the EU.

The problem for and with European defense is that it is more about the search for European political identity than meaningful capability and Yugoslavia reveals that. Reality is not meant to intervene; at least not just yet. The US and UK insist that NATO remain at the heart of European security, whereas the French, with German support, are slowly building a cobweb of security and defense institutions and links with Paris at the center to strengthen their political position in Europe. Key to the French strategy is Germany which, although deeply committed to European integration, is not as yet ready to abandon the Alliance upon which it relied for so long. In a sense the Wars of Yugoslav Succession raise a new German question – which way will Berlin go?

Yugoslavia had long been of concern to both superpowers, worried that its complex mix of ethnic and religious rivalries dating back centuries could trigger a "doomsday scenario," sitting as it does on the dividing line between Slavic and Western cultures. Consequently, although nominally communist, Yugoslavia had always been a semi-detached member of the Soviet bloc under its strong man, Marshal Tito. With superpower overlay now removed, there was little or nothing to prevent those tensions re-surfacing, especially after a hard-line nationalist, Slobodan Milosevic, was elected President of Serbia in May 1989.

The outbreak of war in 1991 also demonstrates the uncertain foundation of European solidarity. Whilst most Europeans want to preserve the viability of the Yugoslav state, Germany breaks ranks and insists upon recognizing the independence of Slovenia and Croatia, even though France and Britain are deeply concerned about the dangers of doing so, given the complex spread of minorities in the Western Balkans. Indeed, on 10 December 1991, for that very reason UN Secretary-General Pérez de Cuellar warns that the selective recognition of the Yugoslav republics might exacerbate the conflict and cause an explosive situation, particularly in Bosnia and Macedonia. The scene for tragedy is now set. On 23 December, Germany finally recognizes Slovenia and Croatia and in effect forces the other Europeans to follow suit. The new Germany is flexing its new muscles.

Furthermore, the new game of great power and institutional politics that is to so complicate the Balkan tragedy is under way. The US does not want to get involved in nation-building, but does not want the Europeans to be too successful. The Europeans are, with the exception of the British, all too happy to try out their new "soft power"[9] but long-used to American leadership unsure about any serious military role if needed. Russia looks on powerless at the agony of other Slavs in a region it once regarded its own. Sadly, the unfolding Balkan tragedy sets the scene for the 1990s, not only in former Yugoslavia, but in Europe and the wider transatlantic relationship. As NATO's pivotal years come to an end, it is clear that squaring the circle of the 1990s will not be easy. The security landscape the Alliance surveys is far from pretty.

If NATO is conspicuous by its absence, the EC is conspicuous by its failure. It is a sorry portent for much that will happen.

### Enlargement and Divergence

The 1990s is also the great age of enlargement, as the Alliance embraces the nations of the former Warsaw Pact. The Soviet collapse leaves a legacy of instability that the Alliance must move quickly to resolve, even if for the Alliance itself the consequences are profound. The former Soviet states want first, American protection, second, NATO membership, third, EU largesse, and in that order, even if, by joining NATO, the Alliance ceases to be the organization prospective members seek to join. It is the new NATO dilemma, but one that must be embraced if the West is to fulfill its historic commitment.

Institutional shadow-boxing ensues. As the 1990s unfold it becomes ever more apparent that for France and Germany, European integration is actually a metaphor for their own power leadership of the European Union, leading to an institutional roller-coaster for European defense, even as the situation in the former Yugoslavia deteriorates. On 19 June, 1992, at the WEU Petersberg Summit in Bonn, Germany, WEU countries adopt the Petersberg Declaration whereby " . . . forces answerable to WEU (FAWEU) can henceforth undertake humanitarian missions, rescue tasks, peacekeeping tasks and the tasks of combat forces in crisis management (including peacemaking)."[10] In June, the WEU holds its first major exercise, and on 1 July a provisional staff is established for Eurocorps, whilst on 10 July the WEU agrees to dispatch a naval force to the Adriatic to prevent the flow of arms to former Yugoslavia.

On 28 August, WEU ministers agree to send a 5000-strong force on a humanitarian mission to the former Yugoslavia, whilst on 14 September, the UN Security Council expands the strength and mandate of the Anglo-French-led UN Protection Force (UNPROFOR). This force had been established on 21 February, to " . . . create the conditions of peace and security required for the negotiation of an overall settlement of the Yugoslav crisis" and to ensure the demilitarization of the three UN Protected Areas (UNPA) and the protection of those residing within them. On 9 October, the UN Security Council establishes a no-fly zone over Bosnia-Herzegovina. Public opinion demands action. The siege of Sarajevo by Bosnian Serb forces and the discovery of Serb death camps dominate the headlines in most Western newspapers.

But the Wars of Yugoslav Succession simply will not go away. During the early phases of the wars many Europeans oscillate between trying to ignore them and offering the parties to the conflict eventual EU membership. There is little stomach for military engagement and it again becomes progressively evident that a continued US presence is vital for European stability. Unfortunately, if most Europeans are on strategic vacation, the United States is also otherwise engaged, particularly so after William Jefferson Clinton is elected President of the United States on 3 November 1992. As the new president had put it so eloquently during the election campaign, "It's the economy, stupid."[11]

Just over a month later, an Austrian tourist and a hotel worker are killed by a bomb attack in Yemen. A little-known group claims responsibility. They are called Al Qaeda.

## Strategy, History and Technology

In January 1993, the departing US Secretary of Defense, a certain Dick Cheney, identifies four critical areas for a US national defense strategy: strategic defense and deterrence; forward presence; crisis response; and reconstitution. Of these four areas only crisis response strikes any real note with the European Allies. Indeed, the divergence between the US and many of the European Allies is not only political and strategic, but becomes driven by a defense technology and investment gap that hampers Allied operations to this day. It is a division that becomes all too apparent when Chancellor Kohl announces German troop cuts well below those agreed in the 1990 Two-Plus-Four Treaty. German re-unification is proving to be too great a drain on the finances of the Federal Republic to sustain a broad defense posture. Ironically, German weakness convinces Paris that their ambitions for European defense will also need to be tempered, at least for the moment. France believes in European defense as a matter of long-held principle but it faces exactly the same dilemma it faced in the 1950s and 1960s. European defense is too focused on institution-building, not military capability and capacity-building, an absence of defense commitment that damages not just the EC, and NATO, but also Frence strategic ambitions.

The German defense dilemma is evident in all European capitals, as the will to act weakens, the need to act grows and yet the capacity to act diminishes. To fill the gaps called for in NATO's Strategic Concept more and more multinational military formations are formed. On 1–2 October, 1992 the Headquarters of the Allied Rapid Reaction Corps is activated in Bielefeld, Germany, comprised mainly of elements from the old British Army of the Rhine (BAOR). That same year Spain, France and Italy create EUROFOR and EUROMARFOR. On 30 March 1993, the Dutch and Germans agree to create a multinational corps. The Dutch are already members of the UK–Netherlands Amphibious Force (UKNAF) and have closely integrated their navy with that of the Belgians.

The dilemma and the paradox of European defense is evident in a pivotal decision by Germany. On 8 April, the German Constitutional Court agrees that *Luftwaffe* aircrew can take part in operations over Bosnia-Herzegovina even though it is outside NATO's area. Little do the Germans know that some ten years later they would find themselves in Afghanistan. It is not an easy decision and causes significant political ructions. It also establishes a precedent whereby as forces are cut, commitments increase. On 21 April, Germany also agrees to send 1600 troops to Somalia. The only way to resolve the paradox of European defense is to harmonize and rationalize the European defense effort, but that is easier said than done. A need made more pressing as the US begins to experiment with Network Centric Warfare (NCW) and military digitization that is well beyond the reach of most Europeans. Consequently, at a meeting of NATO defense ministers on 25–26 May, it is at least agreed to stabilize defense budgets. It is a start.

In spite of self-evident military weakness the complex politics of European defense continues apace. At the Copenhagen European Council on 21–22 June 1993, the EC prepares a report on the future of European security interests and common principles for the future Common Foreign and Security Policy (CFSP). On 22 June, the Belgian Government announces that it will join Eurocorps. Between 21 and 29 October, the WEU carries out Ardente 93 in Italy, a 10,000-strong exercise simulating the rescuing of civilians in a war-torn environment – Yugoslavia. On 5 November, Eurocorps is inaugurated, prompting German Defense Minister Volker Rühe to assert that "Eurocorps is the central building stone for European defense. We are creating an instrument for a joint foreign and security policy of the Europeans. At the end of the road Europe's unification will be waiting."[12] It is a long road.

The reason for such hyperbole is not hard to find. On 1 November, the Treaty on European Union (TEU) enters into force as the European Community becomes the European Union (EU). An annex to the treaty states, "WEU will be developed as the defense component of the European Union and as a means to strengthen the European pillar of the Atlantic Alliance."

For all its political complexity, the creation of the EU offers a juxtaposition to the terrible situation in Bosnia, just a few hundred kilometers from Brussels. On 6 May 1993, the UN Security Council passes Resolution 824 declaring Sarajevo, Tuzla, Zepa, Gorazde, Bihac and Srebrenica safe areas. Slowly NATO finds itself drawn in. It is agreed to combine the NATO and WEU naval forces to better enforce the UN embargo against Serbia and Montenegro. On 10 June, NATO foreign ministers also agree to offer protective air power should UNPROFOR be attacked and the UN request it. It does not impress the Bosnian Serbs who continue their relentless onslaught. On 2 August, the US proposes air strikes against the Bosnian Serbs, which is reluctantly accepted by the NATO Allies. However, the tardy response is by no means all the fault of Europeans. The US remains wary of ground operations, a fear consolidated by the death of eighteen US Rangers in Somalia on 3–4 October and the decision by President Clinton to withdraw US forces from the Horn of Africa by 31 March 1994.

Something else happens in 1993. A group of Islamic fundamentalists try to blow up the World Trade Center . . .

## The Modernization of NATO

However, because NATO was, and is, America's only truly entangling alliance, and thus a leitmotif of US engagement beyond its shores, it is not about to give up on the Alliance. Washington and London, conscious that European defense is mired in institutional politics, move to re-energize NATO. The main objective is the re-organization and modernization of NATO forces around the US Revolution in Military Affairs (RMA) that emerged at the end of the first Gulf War. On 8–9 December 1993, at a NATO defense ministers' meeting, Combined Joint Task Forces (CJTFs) are introduced to create robust, multinational tri-service forces for the conduct of non-Article 5 operations. Ministers stress their commitment "to improving their ability to participate in a range of operations to facilitate closer co-operation between NATO and the WEU in this field, including the possibility of making Alliance assets available for use in European-led operations following consultation within the Alliance. An aim of the concept of Combined Joint Task Forces is to give further impetus towards achieving this."[13] The statement represents the first formal consideration of the use of NATO assets and capabilities for operations outside the Alliance framework. Washington is becoming increasingly concerned about the "duplication" by Europeans of key strategic assets, given the poor state of European defense budgets. Unfortunately, the sticking point soon becomes apparent: the release mechanism for NATO assets and capabilities. France and the US cannot agree.

At the pivotal NATO Brussels summit on 10–11 January 1994, the gathered Heads of State and Government give their "full support to the development of a European Security and Defense Identity," within the Alliance. However, the delicate relations between NATO and the EU are also succinctly captured: " . . . The emergence of a European Security and Defense Identity will strengthen the European pillar of the Alliance while reinforcing the transatlantic link and will enable European Allies to take greater responsibility for their common security and defense. The Alliance and the European Union share common strategic interests." To that end, the leaders also: " . . . support strengthening the European pillar of the Alliance through the Western European Union, which is being developed as the defense component of the European Union," so that WEU states can utilize the " . . . collective assets of the Alliance," and that CJTF be developed: " . . . as a means to facilitate contingency operations, including operations with participating nations outside the Alliance" should NATO as a whole choose not to act.[14] That is an important caveat as it starts a "NATO-first" stipulation to which Paris strenuously objects.

The Brussels summit also launches the Partnership for Peace (PfP) program, to increase the ability of non-NATO partners to work closely with Alliance forces, and to prepare many of them for eventual membership. However, PfP highlights another dilemma – how to ensure that new members can contribute to crisis management operations, commensurate with their size, capability and NATO's need to be effective. It is an acute dilemma. The Alliance is, after all, founded on task and responsibility sharing, even if the costs of operations "lie where they fall," on members so engaged. Enlargement changes the character of the Alliance as Membership Action Plans (MAPs) and Individual Partnership Programs (IPPs) become the focus for much of the work at NATO Headquarters as enlarging takes on as much importance as doing.

Furthermore, PfP starts just as the Bosnian end-game gets under way. On 5 February, a bomb explodes in the main market square of Sarajevo, killing 68 and wounding more than 200 people. On 9 February, now fully engaged, NATO issues an ultimatum to the Serbs – they must pull back all heavy weapons to a twenty-kilometer exclusion zone around the Bosnian capital and hand them over to UN control by 20 February or face attack. On 28 February, NATO forces shoot down four Serbian Galeb fighter-bombers violating the no-fly zone. As with all things in former Yugoslavia, the end-game is protracted, complicated – and deadly.

## The EU Alternative

By 1994 too many Europeans are happy to free-ride, do not want to spend money on defense and have no stomach for robust crisis management. Indeed, for some of the smaller Europeans it makes perfect economic sense as whatever they spend on defense it will never gain them any real influence over collective security operations that are not vital to their interests. In such an environment, the complex relationship between NATO and the EU further deteriorates as Americans embark on modernization and a lot of Europeans see European defense as an alibi not to, even though the Balkans has demonstrated the need for effective European crisis management. For once, it is a split over which France and the US are on the same side, even if they seek different solutions, as both become frustrated at the irresolution of many Europeans. Both institutional and organizational solutions are sought. On 29 June, the WEU presents a report to NATO on the criteria and modalities for the effective use of Combined Joint Task Forces (CJTFs). Once the North Atlantic Council has approved the use of a CJTF by the WEU, NATO will select a CJTF Headquarters from one of its major subordinate commands and prepare it for deployment. Easy enough. However, the sticking point remains control over the assets and the specific mechanism for the release of NATO assets and capabilities.

On 12 July, speaking at celebrations to mark the de-activation of allied forces in Berlin, Chancellor Kohl specifies the essential problem. Europe, he suggests, needs an America that plays a central role in matters of European security and it is in the US interest that Europe assumes greater responsibility for itself and international security. That same day the German Constitutional Court confirms that German force deployment may be deployed for all UN and NATO operations should there be a parliamentary majority. In effect, the German debate, about the where, when and why of German forces, also becomes the bell-wether for the "out of NATO area debate," as the slowly hardening security environment increases pressure to extend NATO's operational footprint beyond Europe. Two days later, German troops march down the Champs Elysées in Paris for the first time since 1940 as part of the Bastille Day celebrations. The balancing act that Germany must perform between Washington and Paris is there for all to see, but so is the length of journey that Europe has traveled in fifty-four years, – the role the Alliance played in realizing such an historic moment, and the length of journey not yet traveled.

## France's Near "Rapprochement" with NATO

Even in the midst of the Byzantine politics of European defense France never loses its grasp of defense reality. Paris fully recognizes the importance of capabilities and the Balkans tragedy has demonstrated that Europeans will not, for the foreseeable future, be able to provide fully for their own security and defense, whatever Paris might like. The key to European defense becomes the involvement of the powerful, but deeply skeptical, British. The French strategy is simple: push for formalized European defense inside the EU and agree with the British ad hoc arrangements that over time will be institutionalized. It is a strategy very much in the spirit of Jean Monnet, spiced by a touch of Gaullism. The British, for their part, keep the door open, partly because London feels angered by a lack of US support for British forces deployed in Bosnia, and partly because of the first stirrings of a post-Suez British grand strategy.

As part of France's new *démarche*, on 29–30 September 1994, French Defense Minister, François Leotard, suggests a rapprochement between France and military NATO. Unfortunately, the Anglo-French truce does not last for long, nor does that with NATO, but it is the uncertain start of a renewed search for strategic consensus that maintains pace with the slow emergence of big politics and big security in the second half of the 1990s.

In October, UK Foreign Secretary, Douglas Hurd, echoing British concerns about the European Defense Community all those years before, says of EU security and defense ambitions, "Security goes to the heart of the functions of the nation-state", and, " . . . public opinion would not understand or accept it if these responsibilities appeared to have been surrendered to a supranational body, however worthy." Equally, he leaves the door open for more Anglo-French co-operation by adding that " . . . although both countries differ occasionally . . . neither for Britain nor for France is there attraction in a vision of Europe which erodes national identity."[15]

This provokes a tart response from the French. First, President Mitterrand warns of potentially lethal contradictions between northern and southern member-states of the European Union. Moreover, the French Permanent Representative to the WEU warns that the more Europeans depend upon the Alliance's assets, the more they will need to have assets of their own to prevent the political subordination of the EU to NATO. Mitterrand then goes far beyond anything London would be prepared to accept when he publicly wonders about a European nuclear deterrent, followed some days later by his Prime Minister, Alain Juppé, who talks of "dissuasion concertée," a concerted European deterrent. Plus ça change...

Thankfully for the British, France's European partners are no keener on this idea than London, particularly the Germans. However, what MLF European-style demonstrates is that France's strategic ambition for European defense goes way beyond that of Britain's. A point underlined when, on 10 June 1995, France, Italy and Spain launch the *Helios 1A* satellite, the first European military observation satellite system. Washington is particularly concerned France is endeavoring to duplicate American assets and shift the cost of its ambitions on to its European partners, at a time of weak European defense budgets. The launch of *Helios 1A* represents an implicit re-statement of French Gaullist principles that is to inform the presidency of the new French President – Jacques Chirac.

# NATO and the Bosnian End-Game

Between 6 and 16 July 1995, 7000 Bosnian Muslim men are massacred in and around Srebrenica in Bosnia and some 23,000 women and children are deported to Muslim territory. It is part of the most egregious act of ethnic cleansing yet seen during the wars in former Yugoslavia. What is worse, the massacre takes place after poorly supported and poorly led Dutch troops, without a clear mandate, hand over the Srebrenica safe haven to besieging Bosnian Serb forces. Action must be taken. The London Conference of 21 July warns the Bosnian Serbs that " . . . an attack on Gorazde [another UN safe haven] will be met by substantial and decisive airpower." On 26 July, the Zepa safe haven falls to the Bosnian Serb Army.

Finally, on 30 August 1995, after many ceasefires, and many broken promises, and after another mortar attack on civilians in Sarajevo which leaves thirty-eight dead, NATO starts Operation Deliberate Force. Led by the US Air Force, this protracted bombing campaign degrades the ability of Bosnian Serb forces to continue their ethnic cleansing. The credibility of the Alliance, of Europe, the UN and the West is on the line. For Europeans it is all too evident that only when the Americans fully engage are the Bosnian Serbs finally dealt the blow that forces them to the negotiating table. By then over 200,000 people have been killed and it is only by 20 September, after some 3515 sorties by NATO aircraft, that the job is finally done.

The Americans take over. The leaders of all the warring factions are taken to an airfield in Dayton, Ohio, and told they will not leave until peace has been agreed. On 21 November, the "General Framework Agreement on Peace in Bosnia and Herzegovina" is signed. In the final negotiations the leading Europeans are locked out of the map room as the deal is struck by US Ambassador Richard Holbrooke. On 14 December, offering a political fig-leaf to the Europeans, the General Framework Agreement is signed in Paris and on 15 December, the UN Security Council authorizes the deployment of an Implementation Force (IFOR) under NATO, which duly begins its work on 20–21 December, alongside the United Nations Mission in Bosnia and Herzegovina (UNMIBH) and the International Police Task Force (IPTF). Europe is humiliated.

Srebrenica is thus not only the beginning of the end of the Bosnian Serb Army, it is the beginning of the end of strategic vacation. NATO must get back to work.

# 5   The Search for a New Strategic Consensus

- France Tries Again
- NATO, Russia and the Enlargement Game
- The Changing of the Guard
- St Malo and European Strategic Sovereignty
- The Kosovo War
- Power and Divergence

> As Europeans look at the best way to organize their foreign and security co-operation the key is to make sure that any institutional change is consistent with the basic principles that have served the Atlantic partnership for fifty years. This means avoiding what I would call the Three Ds: de-coupling, duplication and discrimination. First, we want to avoid de-coupling: NATO is the expression of the indispensable transatlantic link. It should remain an organization of sovereign allies, where European decision-making is not unhooked from broader alliance decision-making. Second, we want to avoid duplication: defense resources are too scarce for allies to conduct force planning, operate command structures, and make procurement decisions twice – once at NATO and once more at the EU. And third, we want to avoid any discrimination against NATO members who are not EU members.
>
> US Secretary of State, Madeleine K. Albright, *Financial Times*, 7 December 1998[1]

After the Bosnian fiasco Europeans are chastened by the events that have led to such spectacular failure in their own backyard. It is evident that the political ambitions for European defense are well ahead of military reality, or indeed the political willingness of many Europeans to engage in dangerous operations. Given that there is also little appetite in Europe for the kind of expenditures that would realize such a robust capability the choice is simple: better defense integration and co-ordination in the EU, or a new strategic consensus with the US – or both.

This choice is often painted as a split running down the middle of the Atlantic. And, indeed, the US does enjoy a different tradition to the European Allies, even the British. Washington in the 1990s saw its role as a strategic reserve for the world, to be used only in emergencies, and was determined not to become the "world's policeman." In the early 1990s, this seemed on occasions almost akin to the isolationism of the 1920s.[2] Great power imposes great responsibility, and neither Europeans, nor Americans, could get their collective heads around that in the early 1990s. Moreover, the strategic methods are profoundly different. For the American, military firepower and maneuver are the credos, for Europeans it is stabilization and reconstruction. Somewhere in the middle is a working strategic consensus, but the very imbalance in power between the US and its Allies makes such convergence hard to achieve. Unfortunately, the split also extends to within Europe. The two countries that enjoy a strategic tradition, Britain and France, are relatively robust compared with other Europeans about the use of force, and because of their imperial pasts are better prepared for the projected policing roles that peacekeeping and peacemaking demand. However, what British and French lack is sufficient numbers of military personnel and consequently the debate within the Alliance in the second half of the 1990s becomes focused on how to generate sufficient European forces across the conflict spectrum that can carry out both crisis response operations (CROs) and peace support operations (PSOs), and the collective strategic vision and political will to use them. There is logic to this. Not only are such forces in demand, but with enlargement impending, such operations represent the kind of tasks that new members should be able to undertake.

Furthermore, peacekeeping suits many of the older Allies, such as Germany and Italy, who remain on strategic vacation, raiding defense budgets to pay for public services, and in so doing imposing an indirect tax on the other, more robust members. Only the British, French, Americans, and to some extent the Dutch, see peacekeeping as a subset of warfighting, for which all NATO militaries should prepare. By 1996, therefore, both the Alliance and European defense are not so much split, but fractured along political, military, technological, economic, doctrinal, and indeed cultural lines. What all agree is that the Bosnian fiasco has been a wake-up call and change is needed. But what?

## France Tries Again

Not for the first time, France makes the first move. On 17 January 1996, the French ambassador to NATO says France will fully participate in NATO's Military Committee, although not in the Defense Planning Committee (DPC) or the Nuclear Planning Group (NPG). But there is a price. Between 31 January and 2 December new French President Jacques Chirac visits the US where he stresses NATO "reform," meaning automatic European access to NATO assets and capabilities, particularly the Combined Joint Planning Staff (CJPS). To that end, the US and France agree that Combined Joint Task Forces (CJTFs) can also be under non-NATO command, so long as a *prior* decision has been taken by the North Atlantic Council and *all* NATO members. But there is a catch. France is keen to have one umbrella decision prior to any European-led operation, and not have to seek separate decisions each time a request for NATO assets is made. Turkey objects.

To smooth the politics of access the North Atlantic Council in Berlin, on 3–4 June 1996, agrees to reinforce the European Security and Defense Identity (ESDI) within the Alliance, as part of the internal adaptation of NATO, to include a new command structure. It is also agreed to support EU-led operations using NATO assets and capabilities. Berlin-plus is born. It will prove a long and complex process.

Unfortunately, given the fifty years of tension since Suez, Paris and Washington remain deeply mistrustful of each other and it is not long before discord threatens to derail the Berlin-plus proposals. At an informal meeting of NATO defense ministers, on 25–26 September, France threatens not to reintegrate into the NATO military command structure unless two top command positions are given to Europeans, particularly the command of Allied Forces South (AFSOUTH). The US mistakenly takes this to include the US Sixth Fleet. That was not the French intention, but as so often with Paris and Washington a non-argument spirals into confrontation. Moreover, another sub-text runs through this Byzantine debate – information security. Although on 6 May 1996, NATO Secretary-General Javier Solana and Western European Union (WEU) Secretary-General José Cutileiro sign a security agreement setting out the procedures for protecting and safeguarding classified information and material, the Americans remain concerned about the use of classified material they provide, particularly by the French, who they suspect of having leaked NATO intelligence to the Serbs during Operation Deliberate Force.[3]

In May, French Foreign Minister, Hervé de Charette, warns that France will slow its re-integration into NATO's integrated military structure if Europe's role in the Alliance does not obtain a more permanent and autonomous base. It is no coincidence that France and Germany also call for more intense European defense co-operation at the same time. On 9 December, Chancellor Kohl and President Chirac sign an agreement on mutual security and defense in which they state their readiness to undertake a dialog on the role of nuclear deterrence in European defense. Indeed, it is an enduring trait of French diplomacy to offer agreement, only then to change the terms which made agreement possible in the first place, even as they claim nothing has changed. *La France Perfide* works – and as so often the US and the UK are forced to react, rather than lead. However, it does not help the search for strategic consensus, not least because few Europeans are happy with French tactics.

However, the search goes on. On 3 December, the US and EU issue a "New Transatlantic Agenda" in which the respective roles of both NATO and the EU are spelled out. "We are committed to the construction of a new security architecture in which the North Atlantic Treaty Organization, the European Union, the Western European Union, the Organization for Security and Co-operation in Europe and the Council of Europe have complementary and mutually reinforcing roles to play."[4] An EU–US Action Plan is also adopted. Moreover, at the North Atlantic Council (NAC) on 10 December, ministers confirm NATO's readiness to lead a Stabilization Force (SFOR) to succeed the Implementation Force (IFOR) in Bosnia, subject to a UN Security Council mandate. Importantly, they also agree further steps to transform Alliance military capabilities and to prepare for the enlargement summit planned for Madrid in July 1997.

Something else happens. On 13 November, a car bomb explodes outside a building belonging to a US security firm in Riyadh, Saudi Arabia. Nine people die. Al Qaeda is believed to be responsible.

## NATO, Russia and the Enlargement Game

There is also Russia. Russia has never liked NATO enlargement; to Russians the Alliance is an aggressor that threatens Mother Russia. Some Russians still think that. Twentieth-century history and Cold War propaganda take years to fade. Moreover, the sight of all the former Warsaw Pact countries queuing up to join the old enemy puts Russia's own humiliation into stark relief. Moscow has long made it clear that it does not want Western NATO forces stationed on the soil of any new members, an impossible demand of free and sovereign states. Equally, Russia cannot be ignored and the Alliance recognizes the need to massage Russia's bruised ego. Enlargement, after all, is meant to stabilize Europe, not undermine it, and there can be no true security in Europe without Russia.

On 20–21 March 1996, NATO Secretary-General Javier Solana visits Moscow ostensibly to discuss civil emergency co-operation, but also to prepare Russians for NATO's enlargement. Moscow had reacted positively to ESDI at the Berlin Summit, but remains steadfastly opposed to any NATO structures on the territories of the new NATO members: the Czech Republic, Hungary and Poland. They remain flatly opposed to the stationing of NATO forces in the three Baltic states should they become Alliance members.

On 2–3 December 1996, at the OSCE Summit in Lisbon, the Russians make their views well understood at the adoption of the "Declaration on a Common and Comprehensive Security Model for Europe in the 21st Century." Moscow is grandstanding. In an early test for the new Secretary of State, Madeleine Albright, and new Secretary of Defense, William Cohen, they stand by President Clinton's State of the Union call for NATO enlargement to be completed by 1999. Fortunately, Moscow wants something. What matters to the Russians is a special status in Washington that sets them apart from the other Europeans. For what it is worth, Washington is happy to offer such a relationship.

Consequently, on 27 May, "The Founding Act on Mutual Relations, Cooperation and Security between NATO and the Russian Federation" establishes the NATO–Russia Permanent Joint Council (PJC). It is easy to dismiss the Act as of little meaning. However, given the history of NATO and Russia it is an important step to the normalization of relations between the two. Not least because the impending enlargement of the Alliance could tip the balance between a Russia that is part of European security, and a Russia that is a problem for it. The Founding Act " . . . defines the goals and mechanism of consultation, co-operation, joint decision-making and joint action that will constitute the core of the mutual relations between NATO and Russia."[5] It is the high-water mark in NATO–Russia relations, but it opens the way to NATO enlargement.

On 30 May, the concluding meeting of the North Atlantic Co-operation Council (NACC) takes place as its successor, the Euro-Atlantic Partnership Council (EAPC), is inaugurated. The EAPC brings together the nineteen Allies and twenty-seven Partner Countries from Eastern Europe, Central Asia, the Caucasus, as well as traditionally neutral countries, such as Switzerland, Ireland, Finland, Sweden and Austria. NATO's transformation from classical military alliance to comprehensive security organization is almost complete ... but not quite.

On 8–9 June, at the NATO Madrid Summit, the Czech Republic, Hungary and Poland are invited to join the Alliance. On 3 December 1997, the NATO–Russia Permanent Joint Council holds its first meeting of defense ministers, having had its first meeting of foreign ministers on 26 September. In December NATO signs Accession Protocols with the Czech Republic, Hungary and Poland and on 12 March 1999, Poland, the Czech Republic and Hungary become the first former Warsaw Pact countries to join NATO. It is a genuinely historic moment.

## The Changing of the Guard

Three other events take place in 1997 that will have profound implications for the Alliance. First, on 2 May, Tony Blair is elected Prime Minister of Great Britain. Second, on 23 July, Slobodan Milosevic, President of Serbia, becomes President of what is left of Yugoslavia. Third, on 16–17 June, the EU's Amsterdam European Council incorporates the WEU's Petersberg Tasks into the Common Foreign and Security Policy (CFSP), opening the way for the eventual integration of the WEU into the EU. The Council also creates the post of High Representative for the CFSP. The man proposed is none other than NATO Secretary-General, Javier Solana. The political symbolism is there for all to see.

But events are beginning to move beyond Europe. On 15 July, The US Commission to Assess the Ballistic Missile Threat to the United States reports that North Korea, Iran and Iraq would be able to inflict major destruction on the US within about five years of a decision to acquire such a capability. Ten years in the case of Iraq. Ronald Reagan's Strategic Defense Initiative is about to be re-born at the behest of the Chairman of the Commission – one Donald Rumsfeld.

Less than a month later, on 7 August, 257 people are killed and more than 5000 injured in simultaneous bomb blasts against US embassies in Nairobi, Kenya and Dar Es Salaam, Tanzania. Osama Bin Laden and Al Qaeda claim responsibility. In reprisal, on 20 August, President Clinton orders cruise missile attacks on a compound housing Al Qaeda in Afghanistan and a chemicals factory in Sudan.

## St Malo and European Strategic Sovereignty

On 25 October, during a meeting in Portschach, Austria, Tony Blair breathes new life into the search for strategic consensus and demonstrates Britain's returning strategic self-confidence as he makes the most pro-European statement on defense of any British leader since Suez. Speaking of the meeting Prime Minister Blair states that "There was a willingness which the UK obviously shares, for Europe to take a stronger foreign policy and security role . . . A Common Foreign and Security Policy for the European Union is necessary, it is overdue, it is needed and it is high time we got on with trying to engage with formulating it . . . " Dutifully, he adds that " . . . we need to make sure that the institutional mechanism in no way undermines NATO but rather is complementary to it . . . "[6]

There is more. On 3–4 December, in a groundbreaking agreement, the UK and France issue the "St Malo Declaration," which states (very carefully), "The Union [EU] must be given appropriate structures and a capacity for analysis of situations, sources of intelligence, and a capability for relevant strategic planning, without unnecessary duplication, taking account of existing assets of the WEU and the evolution of its relations with the EU. In this regard it will also need to have recourse to suitable military means (European capabilities pre-designated within NATO's European pillar or national or multinational European means outside the NATO framework)."[7] In an effort to move the NATO–EU debate forward, and to provide the bridge between the US and Europe to which it has aspired, not always successfully, the UK lifts its decades-long veto on an autonomous European defense, so long as it is NATO-compatible. It is a gamble. Those in favor of a maximal interpretation of European defense move to capitalize on the British shift. Moreover, whilst Britain and France agree on the need for effective European crisis management, given their shared experience of the 1990s, they are still deeply divided over the *finalité* of European defense. As ever, for Paris the politics of European defense are as important as the substance. For the British it is still capabilities and effectiveness that matter.

On 7 December, US Secretary of State Madeleine Albright makes that very point. Whilst she endorses the Franco-British initiative she says that Europe must avoid the "3Ds": no diminution of NATO, no discrimination against non-EU NATO members, and no duplication of efforts or capabilities. The term "3Ds" is later simplified to "no duplication, no discrimination and no de-coupling."[8] However, on 11–12 December, the European Council "welcomes the new impetus given to the debate on a common European policy on security and defense." A little over a year later, on 13–14 March 1999, the German presidency submits a paper entitled "Strengthening the Common Policy on Security and Defense." For France this is the political green light it has been seeking since the early 1950s to lead Europe towards strategic sovereignty. Soon it will have a powerful ally. On 27 October, Gerhard Schroeder is elected Chancellor of Germany.

Between 9 and 16 December 1998, the UNSCOM inspectors leave Iraq, complaining that their work is being obstructed, and the US and UK launch missile and air strikes to force Iraq to fully comply with UN weapons inspections.

## The Kosovo War

Sadly, Europe is not yet violence-free. In Kosovo, the southern province of Serbia in which ninety percent of the population are of Albanian extraction, tensions have been rising. It is also a region Serbs see as sacred to their national identity. On 9 March 1998, the Contact Group, a relatively new grouping of old-fashioned Great Powers, comprising the foreign ministers of France, Germany, Italy, the Russian Federation, the United Kingdom and the United States, call upon President Milosevic to take rapid and effective steps to stop the violence and engage in a commitment to find a political solution to the issue of Kosovo through dialog. Specifically, the Contact Group demands that all Serb special police units are withdrawn and all action against the civilian population ceases. The Group goes on to say that a solution to the problem must recognize the territorial integrity of Yugoslavia AND take into account the rights of the Kosovo Albanians. It is a seeming impossible balance and, given the situation on the ground, is nigh-on impossible. And so begins the countdown to NATO's only war.

On 31 March, the UN Security Council adopts Resolution 1160, imposing an arms embargo on Yugoslavia, which the EU supports. Throughout May, June and July over 13,000 refugees move over the border into Albania. The whole ghastly experience of Bosnia seems about to repeat itself. On 12 June, the Contact Group calls for an immediate ceasefire, the withdrawal of all Yugoslav and Serbian security forces, the admission of international monitors and fresh talks. That same day NATO launches Operation Determined Falcon over Macedonia, involving 85 aircraft from 13 members to intimidate the Belgrade government. It seems to have little impact. On 24 June, Tony Blair warns that the use of NATO air and ground power remains an option unless Belgrade pulls out of Kosovo. That same day, NATO begins planning for military operations against Yugoslavia, but Russia is implacably opposed. On 24 September, NATO defense ministers give SACEUR, General Wesley Clark, authorization to ask members for the forces necessary to carry out military operations. However, with Russia unshakeably opposed, the Pentagon wrangling over the rules of engagement, and time still needed to build up NATO's strength in the region, the Allies agree to give diplomacy one last chance.

On 6 February 1999, peace talks open at Rambouillet, south of Paris, under the threat of NATO force as the Alliance builds up its capability in the region. On 23 February the talks are adjourned. They resume on 15 March, but whilst Kosovo Albanians accept the West's proposals, the Serbs refuse. On 19 March all international observers are told to leave Kosovo. The final countdown to war begins. On 22 March, US Special Envoy Richard Holbrooke travels to Belgrade in a last-ditch attempt to convince Milosevic to climb down but the wily Serb refuses. Although a specific UN Security Council Resolution authorizing the use of force cannot be obtained, due to both Russian and Chinese objections, on 24 March NATO begins Operation Allied Force. Belgrade responds by declaring a state of war. The Kosovo War has begun.

The war continues to 11 June when the NATO air campaign is suspended and Serbian troops begin their withdrawal from Kosovo as part of the plan that had been brokered by the G-8 back in May, and subsequently agreed by the UN Security Council. On 10 June, Resolution 1244 is adopted by the UN Security Council establishing an international security presence in Kosovo that NATO will lead. But the past still enjoys an eloquence. Russian armor suddenly makes an unexpected move across the border from Bosnia and occupies the airport of Pristina, the Kosovar capital. However, after negotiations between the Russian and British commanders, a modus vivendi is reached. Thereafter, British, French, German, US and Italian troops move into the region and occupy their respective zones as part of NATO's Kosovo Force (KFOR). It is still there.

Ultimately, NATO's Kosovo War is a success because of overwhelming NATO power, and because the Allies again find solidarity in crisis. However, there are some worrying developments. First, the US insists that the war plan for the campaign is developed in the Pentagon, not NATO's Combined and Joint Planning System (CJPS), to avoid "war by committee."[9] Second, the war plan is markedly American-friendly. The US then accuses the European Allies of not having done enough, a partly justified criticism, because of the widening military/technology gap between Americans and Europeans. However, the criticism is only partly justified. The European Allies could have done more and the campaign is as much dictated by a US desire not to get involved on the ground or to take risks with air crew, as it is by European military weakness. Indeed, it is the British, French, Italians and Germans that push for a ground intervention and it is noteworthy that Milosevic only starts to talk seriously when the Europeans begin to mass troops on the Albanian border with Kosovo. That said, NATO acted to effect when it mattered, but divisions remain.

## Power and Divergence

NATO's 1999 Washington Summit and the EU Helsinki Summit come at a pivotal moment in the West's search for a new strategic consensus. On the one hand, the US is beginning to transform its military out of reach of many Europeans. On the other, the emerging big security picture is slowly restoring great power to the fore, causing the question of its organization, focus and application to once again become the stuff of international relations.

Consequently, both the two summits are the first real power summits since the end of the Cold War, even if they are replete with both American and European strategic contradictions, precisely *because* they are about the organization of power. Indeed, whilst one concerns the rehabilitation of an enduring, American-led European security power hub, the other concerns the drive to create a new European power hub, albeit fissured by the politics of weakness. That is the state of play in transatlantic security relations in 1999. Equally, whilst NATO's strategic landscape has changed beyond all recognition since 1949, the relationships between the Alliance's founding members bear a striking resemblance. The US is still the indispensable nation, but enjoys nothing like the control or influence it once did within the Alliance. The UK is still America's indispensable European ally, but is re-shaping national grand strategy for the first time since 1956. France is France. Brilliant, visionary and frustrated by the facts of European defense life. Those who share the French vision, either in whole or in part, are some of the weakest European military powers. Those that do not are amongst the strongest. The Soviet Union is no more, but Russia continues to be an at best prickly partner. Germany is once again re-united and is a model European democracy, but unsure as to its security and defense role. The rest? They try to strike a balance between the demands of the US, their own now-ingrained habit of free-riding, and the reluctance of their peoples to do anything too dangerous. For the three former Warsaw Pact countries that are now

NATO members, and the six waiting in the wings, the Alliance they are joining is not the Alliance they expected. It is an interesting moment to audit NATO's past, present and future – fifty years on.

So it is, with the Kosovo War under way, that the Alliance's Heads of State and Government gather in Washington on 23 April 1999 to mark the fiftieth anniversary of the signing of the North Atlantic Treaty. Javier Solana is still NATO Secretary-General, but widely expected to take over as High Representative of the CFSP. The search for a new Secretary-General is under way, with the British Defense Secretary George Robertson tipped as favorite. Fifty years on there is a certain historical symmetry, as the first Secretary-General, Bruce Ismay, was also British. NATO had, after all, been a British idea.

The final communiqué of NATO's Washington Summit reflects both the high and low politics of Alliance life. Inspired by events in Kosovo, an American desire to avoid nation-building, European political ambitions and European military weakness, Americans finally reconcile EU efforts to build up its own security and defense, so long as such EU-led missions are separable but not separate from the Alliance. Capabilities becomes the American creed. That, in turn, raises an important question for Europeans. How hard are they prepared to work to keep the US engaged in their own security? It is a question that will split the Alliance asunder a few years hence, but it is nonetheless apparent even in 1999. Indeed, by 1999 America, and much of Europe, simply do not share the same strategic view. In fact, quite a few Europeans have no strategic view at all, which is why so many of them find comfort in what they think is a purely regional EU security and defense policy with an emphasis very firmly on soft power.

However, what emerges is a new Strategic Concept that reflects the inescapable deterioration of the strategic environment; and the challenges NATO must face as the Alliance endeavors to reach across the collective defense, collective security spectrum. To that end the 1999 Strategic Concept it first confirms that the Alliance's "essential and enduring purpose"[10] is to safeguard the freedom and security of its members through both political and military means, by affirming democracy, human rights, and the rule of law and expressing the commitment of the Allies, not only to common defense, but to the peace and stability of the wider Euro-Atlantic area.

The Strategic Concept then outlines the tasks that the Alliance will have to undertake in pursuit of its grand strategic mission. Collective defense remains the cornerstone of solidarity upon which the Alliance is founded, but grafted on is the crisis management and partnership role vital to the security of the Euro-Atlantic Security Community. It also confirms the finding of its 1991 predecessor that the threat of general war has all but disappeared from Europe, but that other risks pose challenges far more pressing than in 1991 – ethnic conflict, human rights abuses, political instability, economic fragility and the spread of nuclear, biological and chemical weapons and their means of delivery. In effect, the 1999 Strategic Concept lays out the blueprint for the twenty-first-century NATO.

It is a comprehensive approach to security and defense that emphasizes in its scope the centrality of the transatlantic link and the indivisibility of European and North American security; the maintenance of effective military capabilities that will be vital for effective operations, "from collective defense to crisis response operations";[11] and the development of the European Security and Defense Identity, building upon the Berlin-plus formula and emphasizing close co-operation between NATO, the WEU and "if and when appropriate," the EU. It also reinforces the need for conflict prevention and crisis management operations, such as those in Bosnia and Kosovo which remain "a key aspect of NATO's contribution to Euro-Atlantic peace and security";[12] partnership, co-operation and dialog, both in Europe and beyond, particularly the Euro-Atlantic Partnership Council, the Partnership for Peace, the special relationships with Russia and Ukraine and the Mediterranean Dialog; enlargement, and arms control disarmament and non-proliferation.

Unfortunately, NATO cannot escape the European defense paradox; the more the tasks, the less the resources. Indeed, Banquo's ghost is always present in the form of missing capabilities. In an attempt to lay Banquo to rest, the Defense Capabilities Initiative (DCI) is launched to prepare the European Allies for the challenges ahead. DCI is, in effect, an American test of European seriousness involving five overlapping areas for improvement: mobility and deployability, sustainability, survivability and interoperability, with some 58 separate shortfall categories.

But NATO is not the only show in town. At the EU's European Council in Helsinki on 10–11 December 1999, the Helsinki Headline Goal (HHG) commits the EU by 2003 to be able to deploy within sixty days and sustain for up to one year a force of 50,000 to 60,000 personnel, capable of undertaking the full range of Petersberg Tasks. A standing Political and Security Committee (PSC) is to be established to provide strategic political guidance during crises, together with a Military Committee (EUMC) made up of national chiefs of defense staff (CHODs) or their representatives, together with a military staff. EU leaders, conscious of complex crisis management, also call on the

European Commission to create a civilian rapid reaction capability and pledge the capabilities necessary to ensure effectiveness. In particular, echoing NATO's Washington Summit, they call for forces that are deployable, sustainable, interoperable, flexible, mobile, and survivable. The European Security and Defense Policy (ESDP) is formally inaugurated.

The EU leaders also call for appropriate arrangements for consultation, co-operation and transparency between the EU and NATO, and for the necessary dialog, consultation and co-operation with non-EU members of NATO. The key issue becomes complementarity between NATO and the EU.

On 15 June 2001, newly elected President George W. Bush delivers a speech in Warsaw in which he addresses that issue head on. "I believe in NATO membership for all of Europe's democracies that seek it and are ready to share the responsibilities that NATO brings ... All nations should understand that there is no conflict between membership of NATO and membership of the European Union." Echoing Eisenhower many years before, he goes on, "My nation welcomes the consolidation of European unity, and the stability it brings. We welcome a greater role for the EU in European security . . . " However, there is a sting in the tail. European security must be " . . . properly integrated with NATO." And in exhorting Europeans to look outward he asserts that " . . . the basis for our mutual security must move beyond Cold War doctrines . . . We must confront the shared security threats of regimes that thrive by creating instability, that are ambitious for weapons of mass destruction, and are dangerously unpredictable. In Europe, you are closer to these challenges than the United States. You see the lightning well before we hear the thunder. Only together, however, can we confront the emerging threats of a changing world."[13]

America was about to see lightning and to hear the thunder in a way no European ever imagined.

# 6  NATO Today

> The Parties will consult together whenever, in the opinion of any
> of them, the territorial integrity, political independence or security
> of any of the Parties is threatened.
>
> Article 4, the North Atlantic Treaty, Washington, 4 April 1949[1]

NATO today is a strategic security and defense hub that can project
both military and partnership power worldwide. However, the job of
today's Alliance is as it ever was: to safeguard the freedom and security
of its member nations through political and security means founded
upon the values of democracy, liberty, rule of law and the peaceful
resolution of disputes. To that end, NATO provides a strategic forum
for consultations between North Americans and Europeans on security issues of common concern and the facility for taking joint action
to deal with them. Even today, an attack upon one member is an

attack on all. However, in an age where crisis management tops most security agendas, rather than territorial defense, NATO acts as a vital strategic and regional stabilizer enabling diplomacy through robust military capabilities. Today's NATO is constructed around four objectives. First, NATO is transforming the militaries of its members to cope with a rapidly changing strategic environment. Second, the Alliance is expanding its operations and missions, both in pursuit of stability and to counter terrorism. Third, NATO is adapting its forces to cope with the challenges posed by terrorism, failed states and the proliferation of weapons of mass destruction and opening them to new partners, both civil and military. Fourth, the further development of a working partnership with the European Union.

## The NATO Basics

NATO has twenty-six members: Belgium, Bulgaria, Canada, Czech Republic, Denmark, Estonia, France, Germany, Greece, Hungary, Iceland, Italy, Latvia, Lithuania, Luxembourg, the Netherlands, Norway, Poland, Portugal, Romania, Slovakia, Slovenia, Spain, Turkey, the United Kingdom and the United States. However, NATO is a small organization. The total number of people working at NATO Headquarters in Brussels is 3150 (at the year 2000), of which there are 350 members of the international military staff and 1400 national delegates. NATO operates by consensus in that all the twenty-six member-states have to agree before a decision is taken. In addition to the twenty-six members there are twenty-seven Partners, either seeking membership or a security relationship with NATO. There are two major sites, the political center, NATO Headquarters, at Zaventem in the suburbs of Brussels, and Supreme Headquarters Allied Powers Europe (SHAPE) at Mons, also in Belgium. The overall budget for the Alliance was US $133m in the year 2000.[2] Apart from seventeen airborne early-warning aircraft registered to Luxembourg, and the planning and logistics support infrastructure, all assets and capabilities belong to the members.[3] The costs of most operations "lie where they fall" with the members, although a debate is under way about common funding. The cost of the Alliance itself is less than one half percent of the defense budgets of all the members.

## The NATO Committee Structure

In recent years NATO has undergone a major re-organization, reducing the over four hundred committees that the Alliance accumulated during the Cold War. Today's NATO is structured thus. The North Atlantic Council or NAC is the chief political body with powers of decision. It consists of Permanent Representatives at ambassadorial rank of the member-countries, who meet at least once a week. It can meet at a higher level, involving Foreign Ministers, Defense Ministers and Heads of State and Government. The Council is the only body that derives its authority directly from the North Atlantic Treaty. Every other committee supports the NAC. Twice a year the NAC will meet at ministerial level whereas for the rest of the time it is known as the Permanent Council.

The work of the NAC is prepared by subordinate committees, of which the most important is the Senior Political Committee (SPC). The secretariat of the NAC is divided into the Divisions and Offices of the civilian International Staff, the work of which is coordinated by the Executive Secretariat.

The next most senior committee, the Defense Planning Committee (DPC), is also comprised of Permanent Representatives (the Perm Reps) and meets twice a year at ministerial level and deals mainly with defense matters. As its name suggests, it is responsible for all subjects related to collective defense planning and oversees the Integrated Military Structure.

The Nuclear Planning Group or NPG is a forum for defense ministers of countries in the Defense Planning Committee to meet and discuss matters relating to nuclear matters, such as deployment, safety, security and survivability of nuclear weapons, communications and information systems, arms control and nuclear proliferation. However, they do not discuss systems or targeting, which remain firmly under the control of the three nuclear members – the US, UK and France.

There are thirty-five sub-committees supporting the three main committees to ensure national representation in each area where a member participates.

The oddity is the Military Committee (MC) which, although subordinate to the NAC and the Defense Planning Committee, has a special status as the senior military authority in NATO. The day-to-day work of the Military Committee is undertaken by Military Representatives or MilReps acting on behalf of the national Chiefs of Defense or CHODs. The Military Committee oversees the International Military Staff and the Supreme Allied Commanders and recommends to civilian political decision-makers steps that should be taken for the military security of the Alliance. It has often been chaired by outstanding figures, such as General Omar Bradley (US), 1949–50,

Admiral of the Fleet, Earl Mountbatten of Burma (UK), 1960–61 and, inter alia, General Klaus Naumann (Germany), 1996–99.

## NATO Decision-making in a Crisis

Consultation between members plays an important role in crisis management because of the vital need to preserve consensus, which is the cornerstone of NATO decision-making, and achieving rapid decision-making. The principal committees during times of crisis are the North Atlantic Council and the Defense Planning Committee, supported by the Policy Co-ordination Group (PCG), the Political Committee (PC), the Military Committee (MC) and the Senior Civil Emergency Planning Committee (SCEPC).

Decision-making is supported in turn by the NATO Situation Center (SITCEN), which operates continuously, providing real-time intelligence and situation reports on an unfolding crisis. Naturally, supreme authority throughout rests with the North Atlantic Council.

The command flow is as follows. After consultation with national capitals, the NAC will authorize the Secretary-General to deploy NATO forces. The Secretary-General will then issue an ACTION ORDER (ACTORD) to the Supreme Allied Commander (SACEUR) who will then implement the Order of Battle or ORBAT. National forces will then be placed at the disposal of SACEUR through the NATO Command Structure, although they remain under national command at all other times and by and large deploy as national force elements.

## Parliamentary Oversight

Parliamentary oversight is provided by the NATO Parliamentary Assembly (NATO PA) (formerly the North Atlantic Assembly). It is an inter-parliamentary agency providing a forum for Alliance parliamentarians to meet and consider issues of common concern, to build the political consensus upon which NATO is founded. As Alliance membership and partnership programs have expanded over recent years so has the mandate and scope of the Assembly. Today the Parliamentary Assembly has twenty-six NATO members and thirteen Associate members.

In addition to the NATO PA, Atlantic Treaty Associations (ATAs) were created on 18 June 1954 to enable voluntary and non-governmental organizations to support the work of the Alliance.

## Partnerships

Equally, the focus is by no means all on advanced expeditionary operations. NATO's "grand strategy" is to extend its security footprint by opening up the Alliance to new members and building new relationships with key institutions, such as the EU. The specific objective is to enhance stability within Europe, and increasingly beyond, without extending NATO's military influence. This is no easy task, given the neighborhood. The instruments for this more political NATO, and its associated security architecture, are founded upon two programs, the Partnership for Peace program and the Partnership Planning and Review Process or PARP, which prepares potential members through what are known as Individual Partnership Programs (IPPs) and Membership Action Plans or MAPs.

Since the 1997 Madrid Summit a further objective of the Alliance has been to consolidate relations with major partners. Indeed, enhancing security through transparency, consultation and co-operation has been the quid pro quo of the enlargement process and specifically the Euro-Atlantic Partnership Council (EAPC), the NATO–Russia Council and the NATO–Ukraine Commission. There are forty-six members of the EAPC, including the twenty-six NATO members.

## NATO–EU Relations

Relations with the EU are today a vital area of Alliance activities. On 17–18 June 2004, the EU's Brussels European Council agreed " . . . to take forward work on the establishment of a civilian/military cell within the EU Military Staff," at SHAPE, together with formal liaison arrangements between NATO and the EU Military Staff, including " . . . an operations center." EU leaders agreed " . . . that this [operations center] will not be a standing HQ, that the main option for autonomous military operations remains national HQs."[4] EU-led operations are thus reliant upon NATO assets or independent from them depending upon the size, scope and location of the operation.

## The Staff

In 2003 NATO's International Staff was reorganized to better reflect the Alliance's new missions and priorities. The senior political figure in the Alliance is the Secretary-General, who is always a European. The job of the Secretary-General is to prepare the work of the North

Atlantic Council, in his capacity as Vice-Chairman of the NAC, and to act as interface between the Permanent Representatives, and the NATO staff. There have been eleven "Sec-Gens," with the following inauguration dates: Lord Bruce Ismay (UK) 12 March 1952, Paul-Henri Spaak (Belgium) 16 May 1957, Dirk U. Stikker (Netherlands) 21 April 1961, Manlio Brosio (Italy) 1 August 1964, Dr Joseph Luns (Netherlands) 1 October 1971, Lord Peter Carrington (UK) 25 June 1984, Dr Manfred Wörner (Germany – died in office 13 August 1994) 1 July 1988, Willy Claes (Belgium – resigned 21 October, 1995) 17 October 1994, Javier Solana (Spain) 1 December 1995, Lord George Robertson (UK) 14 October 1999, and Jaap de Hoop Scheffer (Netherlands) 5 January 2004.

The Secretary-General is supported by a Deputy Secretary-General and six Assistant Secretary-Generals responsible respectively for the six divisions: Political Affairs and Security Policy, Operations, Defense Policy and Planning, Public Diplomacy and Executive Management. In addition there are five other Principal Officials, the Directors of the Private Office, the Secretary of the Council, the NATO Spokesman, the Director, Policy Planning and the Director, NATO Office of Security.

The International Military Staff is headed by a General/Flag Officer responsible for planning, assessing and recommending policy on military matters for consideration by the Military Committee. Its main center of operations is SHAPE. At the November 2002 Prague Summit, NATO embarked on a new command structure, founded upon the Combined Joint Task Forces or CJTFs, and built around two new major functional strategic commands, Allied Command Operations (ACO) and Allied Command Transformation (ACT). NATO forces are organized around three force types: main defense forces, immediate and rapid Reaction Forces, and augmentation forces.

## NATO Strategic Commands

The NATO strategic commands, Allied Command Operations and Allied Command Transformation, are responsible for the development of defense plans for their respective areas, the determination of force requirements and for the deployment and exercising of the forces under their command. The structure is built around a single strategic command for operations and three subordinate operational-level joint commands in the Netherlands, Naples and Lisbon. These, in turn, provide parent headquarters for two land-based and one sea-based deployable Combined Joint Task Forces (CJTFs).

The principal military officers for Allied Command Operations are the Supreme Allied Commander, Europe (SACEUR), who is always an American, the Deputy Supreme Allied Commander, Europe (DSACEUR), who is always a European, the Chief of Staff at SHAPE, the Deputy Chief of Staff, Operations and the Deputy Chief of Staff, Support. The principal military officers in Allied Command Transformation are the Supreme Allied Commander, Transformation (SACT), who again is always American, and the Deputy Supreme Allied Commander, Transformation (DSACT), again a European.

The SACEUR is chosen by the US President and confirmed by the NAC. The current SACEUR, General James L. Jones, is the first US Marine to hold the post, emphasizing NATO's focus on advanced expeditionary missions, at which the US Marines excel. There is no assigned term for a SACEUR; it can last from one to eight years and he always holds the additional post of Commander of the US European Command (COMUSEUCOM). Prior to General Jones there were thirteen SACEURs, either US Air Force or US Army officers, depending on the emphasis of US and NATO strategy: General Dwight D. Eisenhower, General Matthew B. Ridgway, General Alfred M. Gruenther, General Lauris B. Norstad, General Lyman L. Lemnitzer, General Andrew J. Goodpaster, General Alexander M. Haig, General Bernard W. Rogers, General John R. Gavin, General John M. Shalikashvili, General George A. Joulwan, General Wesley K. Clark, and General Joseph W. Ralston.

## NATO Transformation

Transformation is today's NATO. The transformation of NATO's armed forces is founded on what is known as effect and interoperability.[5] The objective is to ensure transatlantic military interoperability by changing the armed forces of twentieth-century NATO into a twenty-first-century force. In specific terms that means moving Alliance militaries away from static and reactive armed forces, with an emphasis on a regional presence to agile, proactive forces, capable of generating global "effect," built upon precision capabilities, operational coherence and integrated distribution-based logistics, as well as networked intelligence.

The approach of Allied Command Transformation is to create a strategic combined and joint capability that has global reach through network-enabled forces operating at high levels of technical and doctrinal interoperability.[6] The "clothes horse" for transformation is the 21,000-strong NATO Response Force (NRF) that was inaugurated on 15 October 2003 and which reached Full Operational Capability (FOC) in Fall 2006. The NRF is a joint, multinational, technologically advanced force able to deploy in five days and sustainable up to thirty, under the command of Regional Headquarters, Allied Forces North Europe (RHQ AFNORTH). In effect, transformation reaches into every aspect of Alliance activity: organization, policy, doctrine, process, training and education. Above all, it has required of the Alliance a new planning ethos capable of sending forces anywhere, any time for howsoever long. It is a far cry from the NATO of old.

To that end, Allied Command Transformation (ACT) is organized into five key sub-divisions: Strategic Concepts, Policy & Interoperability; Defense Planning; Future Capabilities, Research and Technology; Joint Education & Training; and Joint Experimentation, Exercises & Assessment. Moreover, the priorities of ACT emphasize the drive for change and include transforming NATO's military capabilities; preparing, supporting and sustaining Alliance operations; implementing the NATO Response Force and other deployable capabilities; achieving full operational capability; and, of equal importance, assisting the transformation of partner capabilities. The NRF is the test vehicle whereby NATO's land, sea, air and special operations forces (SOF) can be welded into a single operational package. Moreover, the NRF also helps to co-ordinate national forces at an advanced level of interoperability, to generate what is known as combined effect. In effect, the NRF is a force and systems integrator and thus vital to the development of the effects-based, collaborative, network-enabled and interdependent force of the future Alliance.

## The NATO Force Structure

Capabilities are one thing; organization another. In July 2001, the principles and parameters of the new NATO Force Structure (NFS) were agreed, incorporating all national and multinational forces at the disposal of the Alliance. It is important to make a distinction between the NATO Command Structure and the NATO Force Structure. The NATO Command Structure concerns the command and control of all Alliance forces, i.e. land, sea and air, and is therefore strategic in both reach and scope. In light of the changing environment the NATO Command Structure was first revised in 1997, and again in June 2003. The NATO Force Structure, on the other hand, operates at the tactical level and provides additional command and control capabilities.

Contemporary Alliance force planning recognizes the ever-more-blurred distinction between Article 5 and non-Article 5 operations.

Indeed, the specific objective of the NATO Force Structure is to ensure the capacity to rapidly deploy to crisis areas, both in and out of NATO's area. Consequently, robust crisis response operations are at the very core of NATO's contemporary security projection role, and the NATO Force Structure is most concerned with the effective interoperability of land forces (air and naval/amphibious forces are by definition already very mobile and deployable). Unfortunately, too many of NATO's European land forces remain overly static and of limited strategic use.

The "mobilization" of NATO land forces places a particular emphasis on sufficient numbers of high-readiness, highly trained forces, effective transportation (fast sea and air lift), logistics, capabilities and secure communications. Such a "transformation" also emphasizes professional forces able to operate in all environments, alongside others (interoperability) and over time and distance (sustainability and deployability). One of the most heated debates at present within the Alliance is that concerning specialization versus task sharing. The force ethos of NATO is that all members should share tasks across the conflict spectrum. However, such is the capabilities gap that this goal becomes ever harder to achieve, particularly for the smaller nations. Increasingly, therefore, members seek to carve out niche roles clustered around the broad capabilities of the bigger nations, particularly the US. This particular conundrum is given added impetus by the need to involve Partner nations in crisis response operations (CROs).

NATO forces are designated as either High-Readiness Forces (HRF) or Forces of Lower Readiness (FLR). High-Readiness Forces are those able and available to act at short notice, whereas the purpose of forces with a lower state of readiness is to reinforce and sustain the High-Readiness Forces. The use of such forces requires careful planning and sophisticated command and control arrangements and the Alliance is developing Graduated Readiness Headquarters to that effect. There are six such national HQs that have been assessed and validated, i.e. that have achieved the all-important NATO Standards: the Allied Command Europe Rapid Reaction Corps (ARRC), based at Rheindalen, Germany, with the UK acting as what is known as Framework Nation (i.e. providing core assets, personnel and infrastructure); the Rapid Deployable German–Netherlands Corps HQ, based in Munster, Germany; the Rapid Deployable Italian Corps HQ, at Solbiate Olona, in Italy; the Rapid Deployable Spanish Corps HQ, at Valencia, Spain; the Rapid Deployable Turkish Corps HQ, near Istanbul, Turkey and the Eurocorps HQ in Strasbourg, France.

There are three Forces of Lower Readiness (Land) Headquarters: the Multinational Corps HQ North-East in Szczecin, Poland; the Greek "C" Corps HQ near Thessaloniki, Greece; and the II Polish Corps HQ in Krakow, Poland. In addition there are three High-Readiness Forces (Maritime) Headquarters: Headquarters, Commander Italian Maritime Forces, on board Italy's INS *Garibaldi*; Headquarters, Commander Spanish Maritime Force (HQ COMSPMARFOR) on board Spain's SNS *Castilla*; and Headquarters, Commander United Kingdom Maritime Forces (HQ COMUKMARFOR) on board Britain's HMS *Ark Royal*.

NATO has three research and technology (R&T) bodies: the NATO Undersea Research Center (NURC), the Research and Technology Agency (RTA) and the NATO Consultation, Command and Control Agency (NC3A).

## NATO and Military Capabilities

Also central to the Alliance mission is how best to wring sufficient capabilities out of the European Allies. The specific progress on the 2002 Prague Capabilities Commitment is difficult to assess because most of the material is classified, although there is every reason to believe that such progress roughly concurs with that of the EU's main military capabilities planning document, the EU Force Catalogue for Headline Goal 2010. Therein, of sixty-four Capability Shortfalls and Deficits covering Land, Maritime, Air, Mobility and ISTAR (intelligence, surveillance, target acquisition and reconnaissance), seven have been formally solved, four are showing signs of improvement and fifty-three did not change over the 2002–5 period identified in the EU Force Catalogue and according to the November 2005 Catalogue.[7]

The PCC is designed to support the NATO Force Goals and is built around five broad areas of capability: deployability and mobility; sustainability and logistics; survivability; effective engagement; and consultation, command and control. Moreover, within the general categories, the Allies committed themselves to improving the following: Chemical, Biological, Radiological and Nuclear Defense (CBRN), Intelligence, Surveillance, Target Acquisition and Reconnaissance (ISTAR), air to ground surveillance, command, control, communications and computers (C4), precision-guided munitions (PGMs), suppression of enemy air defenses (SEAD), strategic sea and air lift, air-to-air refueling, deployable combat support and combat service support units.

Progress is again patchy. Binnendijk, Gompert and Kugler in an authoritative 2005 article state that: "At present, much of the HRF [High-Readiness Force] is not adequately capable of projecting power swiftly and performing major combat operation missions in distant areas. Reforming these forces is not beyond reach. The NATO Defense Capability Initiative did not achieve this worthy goal because it was scattered across too many forces and measures, and the Prague Capabilities Commitment evidently is encountering similar troubles."[8]

Thus, in an environment of low defense budgets, creative solutions are at a premium if the Alliance is to fulfill its current and future missions effectively. The figures are sobering. Whilst the US spent $61bn on defense research and development in 2004, NATO Europe spent $8bn. Spending per capita on research and development in the US was $147.20 whilst in Italy it was $3.50, France $48.50 and in the UK $51.80. Defense modernization funding as a percentage of the US investment, per member of the armed forces, ranged from Poland at 6 percent, Germany at 21 percent, the Netherlands at 41 percent, to the UK at 95 percent.[9] What is clear is that the intra-Alliance capabilities gap between the US and its European Allies is never going to be closed and if not guarded against could place NATO's overall cohesion seriously at risk. Co-operability, i.e. working in parallel, rather than interoperability, i.e. working as an integrated system, may have to be the way forward.

Equally, the European Allies are developing a range of innovative solutions that offer at least some hope for future Alliance interoperability. Indeed, the European Allies have no choice but to make better use of what they have and then better acquire what they need. Interesting innovations include, inter alia, the Sealift Co-ordination Center and the European Airlift Co-ordination Center at Eindhoven and the close co-operation between the NATO Working Group and the EU Working Group on air-to-air refueling.

However, severe impediments remain to the generation of capabilities that can enable the advanced global expeditionary or expeditionary stabilization and reconstruction forces that will become NATO's stock in trade. Although the downward spiral in defense expenditure has been halted, only half of NATO Allies and one third of EU member-states spend 2 percent of GDP on defense. The average of all NATO defense expenditure on personnel in 2004 was 52.4 percent. However, whilst the US spent 34.8 percent and the UK 39.4 percent, Belgium spent 73.8 percent, Germany 59.3 percent and the Netherlands 49.8 percent. Professionalization is a must. Equipment budgets reflect a similar story. Whilst the US spent 24.9 percent of defense expenditure on equipment, the UK spent 22.8 percent, France 21.4 percent, the Netherlands 16.4 percent and Belgium (not to pick on Belgium) spent only 5.4 percent.[10]

Too many Europeans retain bloated defense establishments that prevent anything like the 40 percent deployability and 8 percent deployed targets agreed by the Alliance under transformation. Indeed, most Europeans have forces that are, at most, around 10 percent deployable with around 3–4 percent deployed, and that only with the greatest of effort. The Venusberg Group "European Defense Strategy" states that of 1.7m personnel in military uniforms, only around 170,000 can be deployed, with around 50–60,000 deployed at any one time. To say the very least that is a poor return on investment for the European taxpayer of the $200bn or so spent each year on defense.[11] Indeed, spent properly and creatively there is a lot one can do with $200bn before one starts raiding the coffers of social security. But, therein lies the dilemma.

That said, the transformation process is having an effect. Through rationalization Norway is now spending 30 percent of its defense budget on defense investment. Dutch rationalization has increased its deployable combat strength by 2100 troops, with a much more flexible contract for personnel. Germany has closed 105 bases and is reducing personnel rapidly.[12] So long as such savings are re-invested into modernization and transformation (and it is a big if), deployability should improve in time.

## NATO and Future Operations

Twenty-first-century NATO must undertake two vital functions. First, act as the interoperability mechanism with US forces at a very different level of military-technical capability. Second, provide a platform to project European coalitions world-wide in support of the US when the partners choose to act together. For NATO that will mean that almost all operations it takes on will be robust. That old adage of Senator Lugar is still apt: NATO must go out of area or out of business.[13]

Such operations place a particular premium on partnership, robust ones particularly so, because they are microcosms of war, requiring forced entry, pacification and long-term stabilization. That is the lesson of NATO's post-Cold War operations. Moreover, mission success not only requires the application of different types of armed force, but partnerships with other actors crucial to achieving complex political desired end-states. NATO is becoming ever more adept at the planning, application and development of such broad security packages. In the crisis management business hearts and minds matter – not just those of local people, which are of course critical, but also those of the many international organizations (IOs) and non-governmental organizations (NGOs) vital to the management of broad and complex security environments.

To that end, broader-based Peace Support Operations (PSOs) bring together people and institutions that in the past have tended, if not striven, to remain apart. One significant change is the development of civil-military co-operation (CIMIC) and the forced co-operation of diverse people from diverse backgrounds working together for the common good. Unquestionably, NATO can take significant credit for helping to establish mutual respect between the various actors, although it is still very much a work in progress and more needs to be done, such as a clear set of guidelines for governing the relationship between NATO armed forces and NGOs in Afghanistan.

Equally, NATO's renewed strategic role poses six new challenges. First, the neat intellectual boundaries between crisis response operations and warfighting will tend to merge and that will mean Alliance forces capable of operating effectively in all such environments and at all levels. Second, the gap between the military tasks and available Alliance forces is critical. Third, in a world awash with munitions and instability, NATO's armed forces will need to continue to devise new ways of responding to crises before the security environment in any one theater can be stabilized enough for peace support to properly begin. Fourth, with the virtual completion of the European Partnership for Peace (PfP)/enlargement mission NATO needs to be re-focused on its military role. Fifth, the Partnership for Peace program needs to be projected placing NATO at the center of a global network of partnerships, to afford NATO forces more security, capacity and, all-important, regional legitimacy. Current discussions over a Global Partnership are certainly interesting. Sixth, NATO needs continually to adapt its transformation concept to ensure a balance between doctrine, i.e. the way militaries do things, and technology. Too much of the US-led transformation concept tends to sacrifice good old-fashioned basic soldiering, vital in conflict-ridden societies, on the altar of hi-tech wizardry.

NATO Standards are the key and must remain at the core of the twenty-first century Alliance because they are in effect the meeting point of American and European concepts of the use of force (Canada is to all intents and purposes a European country in this regard). The NATO Standardization Organization was founded in 1975 with the specific role of validating the quality of NATO forces, structures and procedures to enhance interoperability between the Allies. This matters because NATO is first and foremost a European organization and effective military multilateralism is dependent on such mechanisms. The US is of course a, if not *the*, vital member, but such is the power of US armed forces, that America will never be part of a coalition – it will lead them, but never be part of them. Understanding that basic truism is vital to understanding NATO's future, which will be to organize Europeans (and increasingly others) into effective coalitions alongside the US in robust operations, any time, anywhere.

The European Union will continue to develop as a security actor in parallel because there will be occasions when Europeans will need to act as Europeans, particularly during small- to medium-sized crises in and around Europe. The Alliance must not be afraid of such "competition." Indeed, the EU will never compete with the Alliance as the generator of global-reach, robust coalitions which will and can only ever be afforded by NATO, and by extension, American power. No current European defense expenditure plans suggest an EU able and willing to take on major operations for sustained periods. Efforts are also needed to make the Berlin-plus arrangements more streamlined and to harmonize NATO's Prague Capabilities Commitment with the EU's European Capabilities Action Plan. However, to speak of the EU as a strategic military competitor is like comparing the England and US cricket teams. Americans may dream one day of beating England, but in any serious competition it is no contest. In any case, whilst the EU plays cricket, NATO will be playing rugby.

## Afghanistan and Iraq: Lessons Learned

There are many lessons being learned from operations in Afghanistan and Iraq. Perhaps the most telling is the sheer difficulty of declaring success. NATO (and EU) operations in Europe, Bosnia, Kosovo, Macedonia, or even beyond in Congo, complex and dangerous though they are, are at the low end of the twenty-first-century crisis response intensity spectrum. If the Alliance is to engage in the rebuilding (and it is a big if) of whole societies torn apart by violence and riven by hatreds, such as Iraq and Afghanistan, then NATO will need more partners and more capabilities to strike a balance between legitimacy and strategic effectiveness. Indeed, three new truisms hold for such operations. First, the further the Alliance goes, the *greater* the need for local legitimacy. Second, the more vital the role of powerful regional actors. Third, the logistics and support for such operations to sustainment combat over time and instance.

So, as NATO goes global its members must be serious about the implications. Indeed, the very real danger exists that the Alliance will talk the talk of global reach stability, and yet be unable to walk the walk. In Afghanistan, even though NATO forces are now actively engaged in operations as part of Stage 4 of ISAF through the extension of Provincial Reconstruction Teams (PRTs), the focus of ISAF operations remains Kabul and the protection of government. For a truly pan-Afghanistan robust peace support operation it is difficult to see where sufficient NATO European forces could be drawn from. The 6000-strong British, Canadian, and Dutch NATO Security Force (NSF) in southern Afghanistan is a bold counter-drugs and counter-terrorism mission, but there must be questions about whether a force of such a size can achieve such a Herculean objective.

In Iraq the situation is even more challenging. Whilst not an Alliance operation, there are many lessons for NATO to draw, not least because the Coalition is trying to create the conditions across the country for effective peace-building in a hostile environment let it be clearly stated; reconstruction in such places takes place during conflict, not afterwards.. Future robust NATO operations beyond Europe are unlikely to be insulated from the kind of insurgency that is under way in Iraq. Force protection must, therefore, be as important as force projection, because it is difficult to justify the sending of NATO's young men and women into such places, except in case of all-out war, without all the tools at their disposal to do the jobs asked of them.

That the Alliance will have to engage in more such operations is highly likely. The globalization of insecurity, information and technology means NATO members cannot turn a blind eye to extremism in whatever form it takes. However, having made that judgment, the implications of such engagements must be fully understood. Indeed, it is where ultimately the Global War on Terror, i.e. the containment of non-traditional threats to Allied security, and crisis response and peace-support merge. In many parts of the world the very stability for which NATO members strive, is the very stability that fundamentalism detests. Therefore, it is important to be clear as to Alliance motivations therein. NATO undertakes robust operations when instability threatens *Alliance* interests and *Alliance* security. In other words, NATO projects security in this post-9/11 world to enhance stability in the hope that such engagement will limit NATO's need to project true force in future. Credibility, legitimacy, capability and capacity are thus the four interlocking pillars of robust future NATO operations.

Therefore, future NATO operations will need to incorporate high levels of planning transparency, allied to the ability to escalate and augment capabilities across a broad spectrum of operations. NATO is certainly geared for such planning and command challenges. However, for NATO European members that will mean getting to grips with the kind of transformation packages implicit in the Prague Capabilities Commitment and fully buying into the work of Allied Command Transformation. There is no way around this.

At the same time, future NATO operations also represent a challenge to the US, which must also adapt its transformation concept. Technology-rich approaches are all very well and good so long as they are relevant and enhance the bulk of the operations undertaken. US forces are amazing warfighters, but the transformation concept around which they are designing their leaner, meaner armed forces is still not matched by the right doctrine to cope with what the British once called imperial policing. Connectivity and capability are vital, but so are forces trained to deal with the human aspects of security. The bulk of missions upon which US forces are currently engaged suggest a lack of connection between the rhetoric and the reality faced by many of the ordinary American soldiers on the ground in places like Iraq. It is encouraging to see the 2006 Quadrennial Defense Review (QDR) beginning to address some of these issues and the extent to which the US has been willing to learn from its British allies, with their four hundred years of imperial experience, is equally encouraging.[14]

In short, the rhetoric of transformation with its need for ever greater precision during military strikes, ever further away from the target with an ever-shorter time between identifying a target and destroying it (and ever fewer troops), too often seems oddly out of place in many of the crises in which NATO needs both capability AND capacity if it is to avoid a force crunch. Transformation is thus a means to an end, not an end in itself. Certainly, it is questionable whether a doctrine focused almost entirely on firepower and decisive maneuver, important though that is, can really be effective on operations that for the most part emphasize policing rather than warfighting. The adaptation of American forces in the light of their current nation-building, policing role is one in which the Alliance can play a significant role. Particularly as the Iraq operation has demonstrated a paradox regarding capability and capacity. Even the 485,000-strong US Army is too small to cope with the extensive policing operation required of it in Iraq, given its other commitments in Europe and Asia. As forces become more professional, as they must, they also become smaller and that creates a real dilemma when the operational tempo reaches a critical point.

Consequently, if Europeans need to transform upwards, as they do, US forces need to transform downwards, with greater emphasis on training for effective, engaged "muddy boots" operations which are the essence of most NATO operations. Indeed, the NATO transformation model should represent the meeting of firepower and maneuver with stabilization, reconstruction, but above all, control. That means getting more expertise across a greater part of the conflict intensity spectrum from each individual Alliance soldier. Twenty-first-century Alliance operations will emphasize the networked multi-tasking multi-intensity soldier, *not* the networked combat specialist.

## Future NATO Operations and the European Dilemma

If for America the problem is one of sufficient numbers and doctrine, for Europeans the problem is numbers *and* technology. Whatever NATO's ambitions for becoming the interoperability nexus for effective robust deployments worldwide, it is not going to work without enough Europeans (and others) that can do the job. Future NATO operations will be very labor- and time-intensive. This will either prevent Europeans from hiding behind narrow rules of engagement and national caveats over the use of their forces, as has been the case for many of them in Afghanistan, or they will simply not deploy. That would tip the Alliance into terminal crisis. Indeed, the old adage that peacekeeping only works when there is a peace to keep is no longer applicable. Future NATO operation will almost certainly involve deploying when conflict prevention has failed and peace has to be made or enforced.

One particular grey area for European armed forces (and there are many) is where peace-enforcing meets warfighting and then lasts for a significant period. The difficulty of managing the crisis in Iraq is demonstrating the very thin dividing line between routine peace-keeping, peace-enforcing and low-end (and not so low-end) warfighting. Even Britain and France find it difficult to sustain such operations over time and distance.[15] Moreover, the ever-increasing operational tempo has further eroded the usability of European forces as the number of missions makes greater demands on static or falling personnel numbers and defense budgets. Europe could contribute at most 30,000 personnel. Europe's most capable army, the British, is a case in point. Nearly one third of the Royal Logistic Corps taking part in "Operation TELIC" in Iraq were Territorial Army or reserve soldiers. This places great strains on part-time forces, the sustained use of which is meant only for national emergencies. The Brits, like all other Europeans, need greater mobility and sustainability with greater numbers, and should avoid simply placing the burden on what are new in effect auxiliary forces.

The British dilemma is repeated in every European NATO member-state, only more so. Effective rapid reaction forces require that at least 40 percent of an overall force be deployable. In 2003 the Dutch were 9 percent deployed, with around 25 percent of their force usable. The Germans were roughly 3.9 percent deployed, with only 12 percent of the force usable, and that is at the very limit of the capacity of the Bundeswehr. The Belgians at 2.8 percent deployed were at their limit, with only 9 percent of the Belgian Army usable on operations. The French have 3.8 percent of their army deployed and could deploy up to 25 percent of their force.[16] Unfortunately, most NATO European members (with the exception of the British and French) are at the end of a defense planning cycle that reflects decisions taken in 1991/2 in the immediate aftermath of the Cold War. At that time defense budgets were cut between 25 percent and 35 percent whilst only limited reforms were undertaken of force structure and capabilities. Consequently, too many NATO militaries remain conscript-heavy and committed to territorial defense, too static for contemporary security and too obsolete for contemporary defense. It will take a significant period of time to generate a robust capability. Consequently, so-called discretionary operations for Europeans too often mean those operations they can do, rather than those they need to do.

Clearly, it is imperative that decisions are taken and commitments made. Indeed, if the forces of NATO Europe are ever to close the gap between the changing security environment which Europe faces and their ability to shape it, Europeans will not only need more forces, but more forces of a new type. The generation of usable, networked, precision and protected forces is vital. That will take time and cost money and for all the rhetoric to the contrary there is very little sign that Europeans have the stomach for such investment.

## NATO Today: Strengths and Weaknesses

NATO remains the indispensable interoperability link between the armed forces of Europe and North America. Moreover, in SHAPE the Alliance has a planning and command mechanism unsurpassed for the generation and management of coalitions, allied to an unrivalled body of combined and joint doctrine. NATO Standards, built up over almost sixty years, represent a body of shared military knowledge hitherto unknown which are highly attractive to potential partners. These are priceless military assets generated over many years of working together. NATO is also a priceless political mechanism, a hub for all institutions engaged in operations, be they civil and/or military and thus represents a critical contribution to effectiveness in managing and responding to crises that those who talk of the demise of the Alliance fail to appreciate.

Equally, NATO cannot escape the political realities of the transatlantic relationship of which it is a part. EU–NATO relations are in urgent need of improvement. There is still an implicit level of competition between the two organizations over who does what, when, why, where, how and with what that wastes so much strategic energy. Europeans stand at the crossroads of capabilities and must first meet and then develop the various capabilities and force level commitments they have made if either NATO or the EU are to play to the full their respective roles. There is only one set of Europeans. More political investment is needed in other agencies vital to Alliance success, particularly the UN Department of Peacekeeping Operations (DPKO) and key non-governmental organizations (NGOs). The deployment of NRF structures and assets in the wake of the Pakistan earthquake disaster and operations in support of the UN and African Union (AU) in Darfur show the extent to which the demand for NATO far outstrips the supply, and NATO's need for partners to ensure the success of Alliance missions.

Consequently, too often NATO must work with too little, too late and far too slowly. That is NATO today – at the strategic crossroads. Ultimately, it is a question of choice. A question of strategic choice. Either Europeans prepare for the big, new world, or they retreat into the Euro-world. Surely, there is only one choice to make – invest now in an effective NATO. The world will not wait much longer.

# 7 The Past, Present and Future of NATO

- NATO – Past, Present and Future
- NATO in a World of Change: Looking to the Future
- Facing Up to New Realities
- Using the Strategic Concept Properly
- Making Transformation Smart
- Creating the Global Partnership
- Making the NATO–EU Relationship Work
- Fighting and Winning the Global War on Terror
- NATO: The Enduring Alliance

The North Atlantic Treaty Organization remains a vital pillar of US foreign policy. The Alliance has been strengthened by expanding its membership and now acts beyond its borders as an instrument for peace and stability in many parts of the world. It has also established partnerships with other key European states, including Russia, Ukraine, and others, further extending NATO's historic transformation. The internal reform of NATO structures, capabilities, and procedures must be accelerated to ensure that NATO is able to carry out its missions effectively. The Alliance's door will also remain open to those countries that aspire for membership and meet NATO standards. Further, NATO must deepen working relationships between and across institutions, as it is doing with the EU, and as it could also do with new institutions. Such relationships offer opportunities for enhancing the distinctive strengths and missions of each organization.

The National Security Strategy of the United States of America, March 2006[1]

The transatlantic relationship was founded to deal with high politics and big security. Thus, the question that today fixates Europeans and

North Americans is, will the change that is ever more apparent in the world lead to a re-constitution of the transatlantic relationship and with it a strategic NATO? After the first age of the Euro-centric Cold War and the second age of the Euro-centric disturbed peace, is the maturing transatlantic relationship on the verge of a third age? The Euro-Atlantic community, far from being the focus of the relationship, becomes the foundation upon which a re-constituted political security identity is re-forged in the face of the many challenges, risks and potential threats that abound.

## NATO – Past, Present and Future

In considering NATO's past, present and future it is worth also considering the strategic landscape into which the Alliance is moving, compared with that from which it emerged. Today's challenges suggest two axes of strategic development: a return to big power politics and the management of strategic asymmetry, but what are the specifics?

*The new deterrence:* Sixty years ago, NATO stood on the verge of the first nuclear age; today the Alliance stands on the verge of the third. The Alliance will need to play a role in the new deterrence that will become the new reality. Indeed, the technology of destruction was the preserve only of the most powerful sixty years ago, but today it is slowly spreading as the non-proliferation regimes that were created for one age, leak and crack in the face of another. Counter-proliferation will necessarily provide vital reinforcement for non-proliferation, but can Europeans and Americans agree on the application of coercion when faced with the fact of WMD threat? They need to because whilst the US continues to offer Europe protective power at the higher end of the conflict spectrum, the European democracies still afford the US its greatest pool of democratic legitimization, and both are needed in the coming struggle.

*China and East Asia:* Sixty years ago China was moving inexorably towards its first revolution, which helped to shape the Cold War. Today, China is undergoing its second revolution, as its neo-communist political elite in Beijing struggles with its neo-capitalist economic elite in Shanghai and Hong Kong. The outcome of this revolution is unclear but, whatever it is, the impact upon the strategic landscape will be profound. Indeed, one country, two systems more accurately describes the inherent tension within China than relations with Taiwan. Make no mistake, the center of gravity of strategic state tension is shifting inexorably towards East and South Asia and the NATO Allies will need to consider the long-term strategic implications of such change.

*The end of post-colonial aspiration:* Sixty years ago the world was on the verge of a wave of reborn and new countries as the retreat from colonialism accelerated. Indeed, part of the price America exacted from its European allies for protection was an accelerated withdrawal from colonialism. Then, as today, issues of governance in the new countries and the role and influence of new elites were pivotal to the hopes of newly independent peoples. Today, many of those elites seem tired and unloved with populations trapped in a spiral of poverty and hopelessness from which fundamentalism and failure are spawned. Political solidarity and consistent engagement will be vital to stabilizing such places but NATO has, as yet, reached no political consensus on the nature and scope of its engagement therein. Indeed, given the current dislike of the US and its Western allies, particularly in the Arab world, regime change, which has traditionally been associated with the desire to remove a hostile regime, could be a fate that befalls states traditionally regarded by the West as allies and friends.

*Russia:* Sixty years ago the Soviet Union was moving beyond alliance into confrontation with the West. Today, the place and role of Russia in European security is once again uncertain and unsure. It is difficult to know whether Russia is part of the Euro-Atlantic community or a problem for it. The leaking of the US battle plan to the Iraqi regime, the dispute with Ukraine over oil and gas supplies and the support for Lukashenka in Belarus do not augur well for the future. Consequently, the newer members of NATO will demand that Article 5 remains in the forefront of Alliance thinking. Russia needs to demonstrate its *bona fides*.

*The United States:* Sixty years ago the United States stood at the center of the world, the inspirational power, leader and protector of democracy the world over, and purveyor of the American dream. The world's most dynamic economy and the undoubted victor of World War Two. Today, the United States seems to stand at the edge of a world about which it seems profoundly uncertain, facing peoples and beliefs for which the grand American idea is as much a threat as an inspiration; rather as the thirteen colonies on the eve of independence stood on the edge of the vast wilderness that would take a century to become America. For the third time in one hundred years the US contemplates how and if it can again make the world safe for democracy. How the US copes with the politics of entanglement in a struggle in which neither victory nor defeat will occur soon or be apparent will be fundamental to the future of the Alliance. The world, and the Alliance, needs a return of inspirational America.

*The European Union:* Sixty years ago the likes of Churchill, Monnet, Schuman, De Gasperi, Spaak and Adenauer were taking the first small fitful steps on a journey to a Europe unrecognizable from the carnage and destruction they surveyed around them. It was a Europe that would emerge from a determination that never again would the Old Continent collapse into self-destruction. However, it was a Europe that had to withdraw into itself to re-build itself, but which now faces a fundamental dilemma – what role if any does Europe play in a world it once dominated? If the world must seem a bleak place viewed from Washington, too often it seems merely abstract when viewed from Brussels. Are Europeans really any longer capable of painting a global mural or have they condemned themselves to forever gaze at Europe's incomplete mosaic?

Two words dominate the emerging security environment, as they did in the early 1950s – big picture. It is a picture that is becoming ever more vivid by the day and which raises several big questions about the future role of the Alliance that must be addressed today, not in five or ten years' time. In this big picture, challenges and threats, such as strategic terrorism, Afghanistan and Iraq, are but parts, albeit important ones.

## NATO in a World of Change: Looking to the Future

So, what must NATO do? Unfortunately, the pace of change is such that so much of the security and defense debate, particularly in Europe, is becoming a *théâtre absurde*, focused determinedly on what can be done, rather than what needs to be done. The world needs strong transatlantic relations and strong transatlantic relations need a strong Europe. They both need a strong NATO. Indeed, Europe can only go strategic as Europe, be it organized through NATO or the EU. That is where France is correct. Unfortunately, as the world gets bigger daily, Europe seems to get smaller daily. In short, European security has become disengaged from world security and that has profound implications for the Alliance. There are, of course, reasons for this. For the first time in five hundred years Europe is neither the center of conflict, nor the source of power, even though the world of today is one that Europeans fought hard to create. Indeed there is a very real danger that a little Europe will lead to a little NATO and thus condemn the West and its system of institutionalized and stable power to inevitable decline.

The center of gravity of power on this planet is moving inexorably eastward and as it does so the nature of power itself is changing. The

Asia–Pacific region brings much that is dynamic and positive to this world, but as yet the rapid change therein is neither stable, nor embedded in the stable institutions the West has built. Until such stabilization is achieved it is the responsibility of North Americans, Europeans, and the institutions they built, to lead the way towards strategic stability and NATO must be central to that. However, such a vision is tough for leaders and planners to generate. Not only is there a marked lack of political will to think big, but the operational tempo ruthlessly emphasizes the here and now, leaving little time and few resources to consider future strategy, missions and beyond. Moreover, telling publics that the strategic vacation is really over will take leadership and courage, neither of which Europe enjoys in abundance.

It should be noted that, at no time in recorded history has the kind of rapid, social, economic and military shift that is taking place today not generated profound insecurity. Tensions *will* arise between states, not just between states and non-state actors, not least because of competition for energy. Make no mistake, the balance of power is returning and with it a range of security policy implications for Europeans, Americans and Canadians that have been absent since the end of the Cold War. Indeed, given the broad array of risks and threats, not only is a new transatlantic strategic dialog vital, but equally a new European strategic dialog. In short, Europeans must begin properly aggregating power, not simply disaggregating leadership. And, they must do so in the context of the political West that remains a vital security identity in the twenty-first century world.

China is clearly the center of gravity of Asian power. In time China could become a vital partner of the Alliance in promoting strategic stability. Shared concerns over the North Korean nuclear program, and maybe even the Iranian one, as well as the purging of piracy on the high seas point in such a direction. However, there are three traits to Chinese military modernization that must be of concern to NATO planners. First, there is much emphasis on disruptive offensive electronic warfare and electronic counter-measures aimed at the US Navy. Second, China is constructing a navy clearly designed to deny the US Navy entry to the Sea of Japan for some two to three weeks should Beijing invade Taiwan. Third, China's defense spending is at least two to three times its officially declared levels.[2] NATO must have a view on this because, in the absence of defense transparency, and in no way demonizing China, the transatlantic partners need to openly and transparently consider the security implications of such emerging military power in a world of self-evident connectivity.[3] China is no democracy.

Furthemore, unfashionable though it is in parts of Washington and Paris, the Alliance *must* be at the center of that dialog. Put simply, both North Americans and Europeans need an institution able and willing to confront high security, and that means NATO. Indeed, if NATO fails, American and European security policy will also fail, and the world will be a far more dangerous place as a consequence. And NATO could fail in the absence of a true strategic vision, real leadership, hard capabilities and security investment.

It will not be easy, particularly for Europeans, and those "other" Europeans – Canadians. There is unlikely to be much money available for security and defense. Indeed, as Asia booms and America extends, Europeans are in danger of becoming a strategic backwater, all too vulnerable to the tidal wave of change with no breakwater to protect them. NATO was once a systemic alliance necessarily *focused* on the Euro-Atlantic area, at a time when Europe *was* the center of the world. Today, NATO must become a systemic alliance *founded* on the Euro-Atlantic area, able to project security beyond its borders, rather than simply ensure it within them.

During the interregnum between big worlds from 1990 to 2001 NATO turned away from its grand strategic mission and lost much of its purpose and cohesion. Today, NATO's destiny is at the strategic level, as a global security mirror of the environment it serves. The Alliance, and its leaders, must therefore reflect on the needs of today's big security environment in which North Americans and Europeans now find themselves and will find themselves. 2016 could well look more like 1946, than 1996.

## Facing Up to New Realities

In effect, NATO must become the security and defense arm of globalization. In this hyper-electronic age, security and defense are merging, creating global interdependence and mutual vulnerability. Indeed, the critical functioning of states or communities of states, such as the Alliance, is now dependent on so many electronically interdependent systems and critical infrastructures that disruption could well be akin to destruction in future. Article 5 still matters. However, like the Alliance itself the treaty that created it must be interpreted as the basis for a dynamic defense in a dynamic age in which borders will be virtual as much as physical. Therefore, the Alliance must go back to first principles and recall why it was formed – to ensure the political and physical integrity of its members through political solidarity, underpinned by credible capability to engender political stability in the face of systemic challenge – whatever that might be. Uncomfortable though that may be for many Europeans, passive defense is no longer sufficient in this world. There will be times when the New Containment requires pre-emptive and preventive operations the world over and NATO must be at the forefront of the development of an effective multilateralism that is willing and able to get tough when needs be.

Given the pace and nature of change in Asia, given the extreme belief systems that seem in many ways a direct corollary of globalization and the spread of massively destructive technologies, much of which are now over half a century old, the only way to protect the international system the West built, is to re-energize the transatlantic relationship with the Alliance at its core. In other words a global Atlantic Alliance. To that end, the Alliance must be allowed to look forward, not constrained by petty rivalries about hierarchy and prestige within the West. Not least because it is vital that Europeans develop a security policy towards Asia and NATO remains the only focus for such a policy.

To that end, it would certainly help if the US and France, or more particularly the Pentagon and the Quai D'Orsay, could get over their sixty-year battle of egos. The rest of the Alliance is mightily bored by their "my idea is bigger than your idea" contest because that for too long has paralyzed the pragmatic development of Europe's security and defense capability in both NATO and the EU. It is indeed strange that the two countries within the Alliance truly capable of generating a big security vision spend so much time being small and petty. It is yesterday's battle. A Franco-American strategic consensus is needed as a matter of urgency.

## Using the Strategic Concept Properly

Some suggest that NATO's Strategic Concept needs re-writing. Certainly, given the nature and pace of change in the world, the context of the Strategic Concept is changing. In fact, the Strategic Concept already has all that is needed to provide guidance to leaders and planners alike as they prepare the Alliance to cope with the emerging big world. The problem, as usual, is political. For too many NATO nations the Strategic Concept is akin to a visit to the Louvre – a once in a lifetime experience. Consequently, there is little connection between the Strategic Concept and the strategic vision, commitment, and hard planning and hard investment required to realize it. The Alliance will clearly need to change the Euro-centrism of the Concept and re-posit it at a global level. In a globalized world, many of the vital security interests of European NATO members now lie well beyond Europe. What is NATO going to do about them?

Unfortunately, without consensus on the Strategic Concept, defense and force planning become unbalanced, resulting in excessively one-dimensional forces that reflect only a partial appreciation of the environment in which they must operate and the missions they must undertake. In other words NATO today. By providing an effective interface between grand strategy and military strategy, a strategic concept worthy of its name will enable Alliance armed forces to re-constitute as change escalates. Political and military realism, therefore, needs to be re-inserted into Alliance planning. Indeed, credible opera-tions at the strategic level require a commitment to strong analysis and force fundamentals and as long as Europeans (and indeed Canadians) only recognize as much threat as they can afford, such realism will be hard to find. Or, to put it another way, until a balance is struck between social security and European security these tendencies will continue. The words ostrich, head and sand come to mind.

Even without a thoroughgoing re-appraisal of a *strategic*, strategic environment the need for a re-think is overdue. Too often the Alliance is being asked to use limited militaries to close a big gap between the securing of interests, i.e. what is vital, and the projection of values, i.e. what is desirable.[4] The smaller the force, the more vital the mission must be. At the very least, re-visiting the Strategic Concept could and should offer a better understanding of the rela-tionship between political desired end-states in complex, faraway places and the use of the NATO Force Structure and NATO mili-taries to that end. Given the ten to fifteen-year lag between vision, planning and capacity, and given the pace of systemic change, plan-ning must start now.

What NATO needs therefore is a Strategic Security Horizons project to match force transformation is matched by transformative thinking. For Europeans that will mean the regenerative transformation of armed forces through better organization and better spending, and a compelling public reason to do so. In short, the linkage between envi-ronment, strategy and capability needs to be re-established. Without such thinking, any alliance, however hallowed, is doomed to subside into irrelevance. It is time to pull the collective finger out and get on with it. The strategic vacation really is over and effective leadership is long overdue.

## Making Transformation Smart

Alongside the review of strategy, the transformation of NATO's armed forces is perhaps the Alliance's most pressing mission. Indeed, the two processes are intrinsically linked. The political credibility of the transatlantic relationship as the foundation of the international system must necessarily be based upon military capability and the military superiority of the democracies. That might not be *politically* correct, but it is certainly *strategically* correct. Unfortunately, the force planning dilemma is undermining NATO's ability to generate security effect in a big world. The need for highly deployable, highly capable armed forces is entirely correct. However, there is also a need for a critical mass of forces that can operate across the conflict spectrum and over both time and distance. Any imbalance leads inexorably to a capabilities-capacity crunch.

Ten years on from Dayton, as NATO moves from regional to strategic stabilization – first through partnership, second through membership and, if necessary, through forced entry and temporary coercion – the Alliance must resolve the resource dilemma created by such missions. In other words, how to balance the *capability* to enter an unstable environment, with the *capacity* to make such an environment stable. If NATO does not resolve this dilemma then it will be saying goodbye to most of its forces for the foreseeable future. Afghanistan comes to mind.

Therefore, NATO not only needs forces capable of undertaking the most robust operations (high end forces), but also forces able to stabilize and reconstruct. Like it or not, some countries are better able than others to forcibly enter, and others more suited to stabilize and re-construct. Such a basic reality has been seemingly lost in the interminable, self-defeating and pointless debate over the much lamented division of labor. There *is* a division of labor within NATO between those countries that can apply robust coercion and those that cannot. Those countries that choose not to, and for quite a few it is a choice, must recognize that the imposition upon them of Alliance membership in NATO's post-enlargement age means that if they cannot go, they will eventually have to go and stay. Equally, much higher value must be accorded to stabilization and reconstruction capabilities within the Alliance political structure. Indeed, the benchmark for political influence has become too focused on network-centric warriors. Every task has its value in the achievement of complex political end-states in dangerous places, in which there are no exit strategies, merely long-term drawdown strategies.

Such a strengthening of strengths would certainly make national defense establishments much more comfortable with transformative planning that for many members is both intimidating and imposing; all too often, preventing effective modernization as transformation collapses under the weight of a welter of excuses about pensions, aging populations, shrinking tax bases etc. etc. Politics is the art of the possible. So is transformation. Or, to put it another way, transformation must be smart and take place across the spectrum of effect, not just the intensity of effect. Transforming the ability of NATO's militaries to undertake all tasks, rather than simply transforming militaries per se.

## The Enhanced NATO: Creating the Global Partnership

The great enlargement mission of the 1990s is over. NATO has by and large fulfilled its promise to make Europe whole and free. In the big new world the Alliance must become the global security enabler and thus the enhanced NATO. To that end, the concept of partnership must change. Indeed, in some ways the political importance of partners will become as important as members. Partnership today no longer simply means preparing others for membership, nor indeed offering third countries a placid political relationship with the Alliance. An active global Partnership for Peace must necessarily place NATO at the center of a world-wide web of like-minded states able to act collectively as an anchor of stability on the international system, expanding Alliance influence and extending those willing and able to join NATO on strategic stabilization missions. An active partnership means cultivating ties with democracies the world over, such as Australia, Brazil, India, Japan, South Korea and South Africa, to name but a few, they must be introduced to NATO standards and doctrine so that operations can be undertaken together without having to re-invent the operational wheel every time. The door should be open to all those wishing to join the global Nato in its strategic stabilization role. If that means a new institution, such a Global Partnership Council or Security Providers Forum then to be it!

Nor is partnership solely about projection. Stabilization starts close to home. Building on the Istanbul Co-operation Initiative (ICI), friends and neighbors need to be assisted, through the new Partnership, to establish best practice in areas such as security governance and security sector reform. To that end, NATO standards should extend to partnership and security, not just membership and the military. It is in the Middle East and Central Asia where first and foremost the new Partnership will be forged or fail. Why? Because the West needs to re-invigorate the state as the organising focus for human security.

## Making the NATO–EU Relationship Work

Institutions are not ends, but means. That means putting both NATO and the EU in their political place and making them work effectively together. Clearly, significant elements of the new transatlantic relationship will necessarily be focused on the new bilateralism of the US–EU relationship. First, strategic stabilization is as much a civilian endeavor, as military. Only the EU can bring European civilian resources and capabilities together that will match the US and thus legitimize the civilian security partnership on both sides of the Atlantic. Second, Europeans suffer from an historical credibility gap, particularly in Africa, as they share a difficult colonial past. The EU can protect Europeans from, or at least limit the charge of neo-colonialism that will inevitably be leveled against them from time to time. Third, Europeans will not be able to project stability, if the resilience of the home base is not protected and strengthened. And, given the range of nations, agencies and bodies involved in European homeland security; the EU is probably best placed to take the lead. Fourth, there will be occasions when America's leading role within the Alliance may be counter-productive in the achievement of a complex political desired end-state. 'The leading role of Europeans in UNIFIL2 in Lebanon will (hopefully) prove to be a case in point. Indeed, one could foresee a range of scenarios in which either NATO or American leadership would probably undermine the political effect of an operation. To that end, the flag one places on an operation is almost as important as the capabilities and capacities one brings to bear. The political identity one projects matters in complex security environments. In the Middle East and Central Asia, to name just two regions of concern, such circumstances will certainly exist and EU leadership could be better placed to generate success, even if EU-led operations rely upon NATO assets and capabilities. It is certainly time for Europeans to step up to the plate.[5]

Put simply, in today's world the EU is as an essential Alliance partner. It is therefore a profound shame that little Europeanization has prevented the alliance of Alliance and Union. The EU needs a strong NATO, and NATO needs a strong EU. It is as simple and straightforward as that. The security engagement of a pluralistic security community in a complex security environment requiring complex responses needs an array of actors and institutions. Diversity is strength. Communication, co-ordination and capability are what matters.

Today, the West has two security leadership hubs – NATO *and* the EU. Depending on the mission, the location or the scale of the crisis to be managed, *either* NATO or the EU will be in the lead. Indeed, if Europeans are to take responsibility for their own security destiny they must become serious security actors and much of that will necessarily take place in the EU. There is a desperate need for both institutions, just as there is room enough for both.

The road to effective co-operation? First, no more pointless grand EU–NATO declarations. A pragmatic relationship between the two organizations needs to be forged based on practical co-operation in the field. NATO–EU Crisis Action Teams (CATs) would be such a first step. Second, there is only one set of Europeans, and only one set of capabilities. A closer working relationship is needed between the Prague Capabilities Commitment (PCC) and the European Capabilities Action Plan (ECAP) as a matter of urgency. Third, the relationship between the NATO Response Force and the EU Battle Groups (BGs) needs to be better established, built around a pool of forces that can be used in either format. The old argument that, if NATO gets too close to the EU the Union will be prevented from developing as a security actor, is as wrong as it is outdated.

## Fighting and Winning the Global War on Terror

Strategic counter-terror is mutating into a sustained conflict. Indeed, history has been kick-started by the Global War on Terror. Afghanistan and Iraq sit on the threshold between counter-terror, strategic stability and strategic coercion and consequently stretch the civil and military means of all Alliance members. Indeed, what is emerging from the counter-offensive is a new Thirty Years War[6] in which extreme belief systems, old but massively destructive technologies, unstable and intolerant societies, strategic crime and the globalization of all commodities and communications combine to create a multi-dimensional threat which transcends geography, function and capability. The response of the West and its partners will require a new grand strategy with a big NATO at its core.

There is a continuum between strategic counter-terrorism and the new big world of states because power politics and prayer politics are ultimately the same. Counter-terrorism must not, therefore, become the be all and end all of Alliance planning or, indeed, an excuse to focus on tactical terrorism and thus avoid the big questions of a big age. Indeed, Alliance strategic thinking and strategic action will require re-generated strategic vision, founded on relevant armed forces capable of managing broad threats in alliance with strategic civil-military capabilities and capacities – a comprehensive approach to security. NATO is the natural locus for such an approach.

## NATO: The Enduring Alliance

Like it or not, Europeans and North Americans are going to have to think (and ultimately act) hard about the world beyond Europe. Like it or not, Europeans are going to have to rehabilitate coercion, if their non-coercive means and tools are to work. Indeed, there is no such thing as soft or hard power, only effect.[7] Like it or not, the Alliance is going to have to do far more with existing resources. Like it or not, all the allies must generate a cost-effective, critical mass of effect in the face of a critical mass of insecurity, instability and strategic change.

The twenty-first century will place a particular premium on credible and effective mechanisms for multiplying security effect, and that means institutions such as NATO and the EU working in harmony for the greater good. Above all, the world needs a strong West and the West needs a big NATO. If the West thinks big now about the big future it faces then the Euro-Atlantic Community stands the best possible chance of saving the international system the West itself created. Alternatively, a lack of strategic vision will condemn to failure the system of institutionalized balance, legitimacy and stability the West gave the world. And one world will be made immeasurably more dangerous as a result. In such circumstances, the West will find itself no longer the master of its own security destiny, but buffeted and damaged by the events only it has the collective power to manage and control. Sadly, too many members of the Alliance seemed to have accepted the inevitability of decline and are simply waiting for it to be administered. That must stop.

Make no mistake, only a strong West will guarantee a stable twenty-first century and prevent the emergence of global hyper-nationalism and the spread of hyper-fundamentalism. One thing is clear: the need for NATO remains as strong as ever, if not stronger, because it is the one organization capable of organizing truly credible, legitimate and stable coercive power in a world marked by instability and even chaos.

The bottom line is this: NATO is only as strong as the sum of its parts. Until those European Allies that play at defense get real then NATO will always be behind the curve. Ultimately it is about making tough choices in a tough world. Familiar excuses will not wash. The environment does not go away and those that make such excuse simply transfer the cost of their security on to those that do not, i.e. the Americans, the British and the French. If there can be no taxation without representation, there can be no representation without commitment. That means willingness to pay a proportionate amount for relevant military forces as part of a proportionate collective security effort. Too many Europeans only free-ride, they free-drive as well. That too must stop.

NATO's journey has been a long one that is only just beginning. The Alliance will remain, but it is up to the members to make it effective. If not they will be failing history. It would not be for the first time. NATO is the enduring alliance. Only time will tell if it remains the effective alliance.

# Appendix
# NATO Timeline, 1949–2005[1]

**1949**
| | |
|---|---|
| 4/49 | North Atlantic Treaty, the founding of NATO |
| 8/49 | North Atlantic Treaty enters into force |
| 9/49 | First session of the North Atlantic Council in Washington |

**1950**
| | |
|---|---|
| 1/50 | President Truman approves plan for integrated defense of Europe |
| 12/50 | General Dwight D. Eisenhower appointed first Supreme Allied Commander, Europe (SACEUR) |

**1951**
| | |
|---|---|
| 4/51 | Supreme Headquarters Allied Powers Europe (SHAPE) becomes operational |

**1952**
| | |
|---|---|
| 2/52 | Greece and Turkey accede to North Atlantic Treaty |
| 3/52 | Lord Bruce Ismay becomes first NATO Secretary-General |

**1954**
| | |
|---|---|
| 5/54 | US and UK reject Soviet bid to join NATO |
| 8/54 | European Defense Community collapses |

**1955**
| | |
|---|---|
| 5/55 | West Germany becomes a NATO member |
| 7/55 | First conference of NATO Parliamentarians |

**1956**
| | |
|---|---|
| 10–11/56 | Suez Crisis |

**1957**
| | |
|---|---|
| 5/57 | Paul-Henri Spaak (Belgium) becomes NATO Secretary-General |
| 10/57 | Sputnik is launched; the missile gap debate starts |
| 12/57 | Heads of State and Government affirm NATO's principles and purposes |

**1958**

4/58    NATO Defense Ministers affirm the defensive nature of the Alliance

11/58   USSR renounces Four-Power Agreement over Berlin

**1959**

12/59   Opening of new NATO HQ in Paris

**1960**

5/60    American U2 spy plane shot down over Soviet territory

11/60   Khrushchev confirms doctrine of peaceful coexistence

**1961**

4/61    Dirk U. Stikker (Netherlands) becomes NATO Secretary-General

8/61    Erection of the Berlin Wall

**1962**

5/62    NATO foreign and defense ministers consider the threshold for the use of nuclear weapons

10–11/62   Cuban Missile Crisis

12/62   US President Kennedy and UK Prime Minister Macmillan agree to contribute part of their strategic nuclear forces to NATO

**1963**

6/63    "Hot-line" established between Moscow and Washington to avoid crises

10/63   14,500 US soldiers are flown from US to Germany as part of Operation Big Lift

**1964**

8/64    Manlio Brosio (Italy) becomes NATO Secretary-General

10/64   Leonid Brezhnev becomes leader of the Soviet Union

**1965**

9/65    President De Gaulle announces France will withdraw from NATO integrated military structure (IMS)

**1966**

3/66    France formally withdraws from the IMS. NATO leaves France

12/66   Defense Planning Committee establishes the Nuclear Planning Group

**1967**

3/67    New SHAPE opened at Mons, Belgium

10/67   New NATO HQ opened in Brussels, Belgium

12/67   Harmel Report on the Future Tasks of the Alliance approved by NATO. Flexible Response adopted

**1968**
6/68 NAC issues Declaration on Mutually Balanced Force Reduction Talks (MBFR)

**1970**
12/70 Defense Planning Committee adopts the study Alliance Defense in the 70s

**1971**
10/71 Joseph Luns (Netherlands) succeeds Manlio Brosio as Secretary-General of NATO

**1972**
6/72 Quadripartite Agreement on Berlin signed

**1973**
10/73 Arab–Israeli Yom Kippur War

**1974**
6/74 NATO Heads of State and Government sign A Declaration on Atlantic Relations

**1976**
12/76 NAC rejects demand from Warsaw Treaty Organization (WTO) that NATO renounce first use of nuclear weapons

**1977**
5/77 NAC initiates Long-Term Defense Program (LTDP) to modernize NATO forces
10/77 NPG establishes High-Level Group (HLG) on theater nuclear force modernization

**1979**
4/79 Establishment of Special Group to study arms control aspects of theater nuclear systems
12/79 Dual-Track decision to deploy Cruise and Pershing missiles and seek a negotiated compromise with Moscow
Soviet invasion of Afghanistan

**1981**
11/81 President Reagan announces Intermediate Range Nuclear Force Talks (INF) and Strategic Arms Reduction Talks (START) with the Soviets

**1982**
6/82 Spain becomes the sixteenth member of NATO NAC issues the Bonn Declaration, setting out the Alliance Program for Peace in Freedom

**1983**
3/83 President Reagan announces the Strategic Defense Initiative to protect the US against missile strike
11/83 Cruise and Pershing missiles begin to be deployed

**1984**

6/84      Lord Peter Carrington (UK) becomes NATO Secretary-General

**1985**

3/85      Mikhail Gorbachev becomes leader of the Soviet Union

**1986**

11/86     NATO Foreign Ministers issue the Brussels Declaration on Conventional Arms Control to eliminate disparities from the Atlantic to the Urals

**1987**

12/87     President Reagan and Soviet leader Gorbachev sign the INF Treaty

**1988**

7/88      Manfred Woerner (Ger) becomes NATO Secretary-General

**1989**

4/89      Fortieth anniversary celebrations of the founding of the Alliance

5/89      NAC confirms major initiative for conventional force reductions in Europe

11/89     The Berlin Wall falls

**1990**

7/90      NATO Heads of State and Government issue the London Declaration on a Transformed Atlantic Alliance, agree a New Strategic Concept and outline plans for cooperation with Central and Eastern European countries

8/90      Iraq invades Kuwait

**1991**

3/91      Coalition victory in First Gulf War

6/91      NATO foreign ministers issue statement on Partnership with the countries of Central and Eastern Europe, NATO's Core Security Functions and the resolution of problems with the CFE Treaty

10/91     NATO defense ministers reduce stockpiles of sub-strategic nuclear weapons by 80 percent

12/91     NATO defense ministers review major changes in NATO force structure

**1992**

3/92      Extraordinary meeting of the North Atlantic Cooperation Council agrees a Work Plan for Dialogue, Partnership and Cooperation

5/92      First formal meeting of NAC with the Western European Union Council

| | |
|---|---|
| 7/92 | CFE Treaty signed |
| 9/92 | NAC agrees measures to support UN, CSCE and EC bring peace to former Yugoslavia |
| 10/92 | NATO's new Allied Command Europe Rapid Reaction Corps inaugurated |
| 11/92 | NATO supplies UNPROFOR with an operational headquarters in Bosnia |
| 12/92 | Foreign ministers' meeting of the North Atlantic Council (NAC) agrees to strengthen NATO peacekeeping |

**1993**

| | |
|---|---|
| 1/93 | Agreement over use of Eurocorps within Alliance framework |
| 4/93 | NAC begins enforcing no-fly zone in Bosnia |
| 12/93 | Ministerial NAC discusses proposals for Partnership for Peace |

**1994**

| | |
|---|---|
| 1/94 | NATO Brussels Summit; Alliance Heads of State and Government launch Partnership for Peace, Combined Joint Task Forces (CJTF) and the development of a European Security and Defense Identity (ESDI) |
| 8/94 | NATO forces attack Bosnian Serb forces in the Sarajevo Exclusion Zone |
| | NATO Secretary-General Manfred Woerner dies |
| 10/94 | Willy Claes (Belgium) becomes NATO Secretary-General |

**1995**

| | |
|---|---|
| 1/95 | NAC agrees a NATO Standardization Organization covering material, technical and operational standardization |
| 7/95 | Bosnian Serb forces attack Srebrenica, a UN Safe Haven |
| 8/95 | NATO launches Operation Deliberate Force against Bosnian Serb forces |
| 9/95 | NATO ambassadors approve a Study on NATO Enlargement |
| 10/95 | Willy Claes resigns as NATO Secretary-General |
| 11/95 | Dayton Peace Talks start over Bosnia |
| 12/95 | Javier Solana Madariaga (Spain) becomes NATO Secretary-General |
| | NATO formally endorses deployment of 60,000 troops as part of the Implementation Force (IFOR) to Bosnia |

**1996**

| | |
|---|---|
| 6/96 | NATO Berlin Summit agrees to strengthen the ESDI as part of the internal adaptation of NATO |
| 12/96 | NAC meeting confirms NATO's readiness to lead a Stabilization Force (SFOR) to Bosnia, as well as the internal and external transformation of the Alliance |

**1997**

2/97    NATO proposes major changes to the CFE Treaty to stabilize conventional forces in post-Cold War Europe

5/97    Signing of the Founding Act on Mutual Relations, Co-operation and Security between NATO and Russia

Concluding meeting of North Atlantic Co-operation Council (NACC) and inaugural meeting of Euro-Atlantic Partnership Council (EAPC)

7/97    First meeting of NATO–Russia Permanent Joint Council (PJC)

Madrid Summit: NATO Heads of State and Government agree to invite the Czech Republic, Hungary and Poland to join in 1999

**1998**

3/98    NAC issues statement expressing concern over upswing in violence in Kosovo

10/98   NATO issues activation orders (ACTORDs) for limited air strikes against Yugoslavia. It is one step short of action

12/98   NAC agrees to update the Strategic Concept

NATO ministers approve the 1998 Ministerial Guidance providing political guidance to NATO Military Authorities up to 2006

**1999**

3/99    NATO initiates air strikes again in Yugoslavia aimed at halting the violence in Kosovo

4/99    Washington Summit: NATO celebrates 50 years and work begins on preparing the Alliance for the challenges posed by the twenty-first century. They also launch the adapted Strategic Concept, review the situation in Kosovo, consider the internal adaptation of the Alliance and Ukraine's contribution to stability in Europe and launch the Defense Capabilities Initiative

6/99    NATO operations are suspended in Yugoslavia and the UN Security Council authorizes the deployment of the NATO-led Kosovo Force (KFOR)

10/99   Lord George Robertson (UK) becomes NATO Secretary-General

12/99   NATO Foreign Ministers meet to discuss implications of EU's European Security and Defense Policy (ESDP)

**2000**

9/00    First meeting of the NAC and the interim Political and Security Committee of the EU

| 12/00 | NATO defense ministers adopt a five-year force plan to address requirements of the new security environment |
|---|---|

**2001**

| 3/01 | Lord Robertson, together with EU High Representative Javier Solana, visit Skopje, Former Yugoslav Republic of Macedonia (FYROM) as situation therein deteriorates |
|---|---|
| 6/01 | At NATO defense ministers meeting new US Defense Secretary, Donald Rumsfeld, argues for Allied Missile Defense (AMD)<br>President Bush in a Warsaw speech calls for the further integration of Central and Eastern European countries in NATO and for Europeans to take on more security responsibilities |
| 8/01 | NATO launches 3500-strong Operation Essential Harvest to FYROM to collect and destroy rebel weapons |
| 9/01 | Al Qaeda attacks Washington and New York<br>For the first time in its history NATO invokes Article 5 of the North Atlantic Treaty, the collective defense cornerstone of the Alliance in support of the US |
| 11/01 | US coalition commences operations against Afghanistan |
| 12/01 | NATO defense ministers meet to discuss how to adapt NATO to the Global War on Terror (GWOT) and increase the Alliance's ability to project NATO forces globally |

**2002**

| 11/02 | Prague Summit: Bulgaria, Estonia, Latvia, Lithuania, Romania, Slovakia and Slovenia are invited to join NATO. The Prague Capabilities Commitment (PCC) replaces the DCI and it is agreed to set up a 21,000-strong NATO Response Force (NRF) |
|---|---|
| 12/02 | NATO and the EU sign The EU–NATO Declaration on ESDP providing for EU access to NATO assets and capabilities. Berlin-plus is finally activated some six years after first agreed |

**2003**

| 2/03 | Turkey invokes Article 4 of the North Atlantic Treaty believing itself threatened by the situation in Iraq<br>Bypassing French objections, the Defense Planning Committee authorizes the deployment of NATO AWACs, and missile, chemical and biological defenses to Turkey |
|---|---|
| 3/03 | EU formally adopts the Berlin-plus agenda and signs a NATO–EU agreement on Security of (classified) Information. |

A Comprehensive Framework for EU–NATO Permanent Arrangements is also finalized

The Iraq War starts

8/03 NATO takes over control of the International Security Assistance Force (ISAF) in Afghanistan

**2004**

3/04 A series of bomb attacks on commuter trains in Madrid kills 191 people

6/04 Istanbul Summit: NATO Heads of State and Government agree to expand ISAF in Afghanistan, to conclude operations in Bosnia, to offer training assistance to Iraq, to enhance Operation Active Endeavour in the Mediterranean, to enhance their capacity to fight terrorism and to expand the Mediterranean Dialogue to the broader Middle East through the Istanbul Cooperation Initiative

12/04 EU Operation Althea is launched in Bosnia, replacing NATO's SFOR

NATO–Russia Council agree an action plan against terrorism

**2005**

3/05 NATO defense ministers agree to take over full command of ISAF in Afghanistan and review the ability of the Alliance to undertake complex operations, including the planning and financing of operations, decision-making and the "usability" and deployability of Alliance forces

12/05 NATO foreign ministers discuss Stage 3 of ISAF, expanding into the south of Afghanistan as part of a NATO Security Force (NSF) to be led by the British. This expands ISAF from 9000 to 15000

# Notes

**Foreword**

1 Julian Lindley-French and Katja Flückiger, *A Chronology of European Security and Defence 1945–2005* (Geneva: Geneva Center for Security Policy, 2005).

**1 A World Gone Mad: 9/11 and Iraq**

1 Julian Lindley-French and Katja Flückiger, *A Chronology of European Security and Defence 1945–2005* (Geneva: Geneva Center for Security Policy, 2005), 229.
2 In 1812 the British burnt down the White House.
3 *Le Monde*, editorial, 12 September 2001.
4 The European Council, "September 11, 2001: Attack on America, Report of the Extraordinary European Council Meeting"; 21 September 2001, www.yale.edu/lawweb/avalon/sept_11.
5 Operation Eagle Assist involved the control of American skies by NATO AWAC aircraft crewed by 830 personnel from thirteen NATO nations, flying some 4300 hours on 360 operational sorties.
6 European Council, Laeken, 14–15 December 2001. See Maartje Rutten, ed., "From Nice to Laeken – European Defense: Core Documents," Volume II, *Chaillot Papers* 51 (Paris: European Union – Institute for Security Studies, 2001), 185.
7 Lindley-French and Flückiger, *A Chronology of European Security and Defence 1945–2005*, 230.
8 After a 1960s song written by Paul Anka, and made famous by Frank Sinatra.
9 European Council, Barcelona Presidency Conclusions. See Rem Korteweg, *The Discourse on European Defence* (The Hague: Clingendael Center for Strategic Studies – Netherlands Institute for International Relations, 2005), 33.
10 Sir Christopher Meyer, the British Ambassador to Washington, says, "The speech was Blair's doctrine of pre-emption. The lesson of 9/11 was . . . that you did not wait to be hit if you saw a threat coming. You dealt with it before it materialized. Saddam Hussein was such a threat. Doing nothing

about him was not an option." Christopher Meyer, *DC Confidential* (London: Weidenfeld & Nicolson, 2005), 247.

11  Lindley-French and Flückiger, *A Chronology of European Security and Defence 1945–2005*, 234.

12  "We are steadfast in our commitment to the transatlantic link, to NATO's fundamental security tasks; to our shared democratic values; and to the United Nations Charter." Prague Summit Declaration issued by the Heads of State and Government participating in the meeting of the North Atlantic Council in Prague on 21 November 2002, http://www.nato.int/docu/pr/2002/p02–127e.htm.

13  Presidency Conclusions, Copenhagen European Council, 12–13 December 2002, from Jean-Yves Haines, ed., "From Laeken to Copenhagen – European Defense: Core Documents," *Chaillot Papers* 57 (Paris: European Union – Institute for Security Studies, 2003), 170.

14  www.heritage.org/Research/NationalSecurity.

15  The European Union, *A Secure Europe in a Better World: The European Security Strategy* (Paris: The European Union – Institute for Security Studies, 2003), 20.

16  "The Istanbul Declaration, Our Security in a New Era, issued by the Heads of State and Government participating in the meeting of the North Atlantic Council in Istanbul on 28 June 2004," NATO Press Release 2004 (097), 28 June 2004, http://www.nato.int/docu/pr/2004/p04–097e.htm.

17  J. M. and M. J. Cohen, eds, *The Penguin Dictionary of Quotations* (London: Godfrey Cave Associates Ltd, 1986), 111.

## 2  Facing the Enemy

1  *NATO Handbook* (Brussels: NATO Office of Information and Press, 2001), 528.

2  George Washington had warned against such alliances when he said in his farewell address on 17 September 1796, "It is our true policy to steer clear of permanent alliance with any portion of the foreign world." J. M and M. J. Cohen, eds, *The Penguin Dictionary of Quotations* (London: Godfrey Cave Associates Ltd, 1986), 410.

3  Kennan wrote, "In this [communist] dogma, with its basic altruism of purpose, they found justification for their instinctive fear of the outside world, for the dictatorship without which they did not know how to rule, for cruelties they did not dare to inflict, for sacrifices they felt bound to demand. In the name of Marxism they sacrificed every single ethical value in their methods and tactics." George F. Kennan, "Long Telegram," 22 February 1946, reprinted in Henry Kissinger, *Diplomacy* (New York: Simon & Schuster, 1994), 447.

4  The five signatories expressed their determination "to take any and all steps which might become necessary should there be a return to a German policy of aggression." See Alfred Grosser, ed., *The Western Alliance: European–American Relations since 1945* (London: Macmillan, 1980), 85.

5  Julian Lindley-French and Katja Flückiger, *A Chronology of European Security and Defence 1945–2005* (Geneva: Geneva Center for Security Policy, 2005), 23.

6 "The Declaration of 9 May 1950" (The Schuman Declaration), http://europa.eu.int/comm/publications/booklets/eu_documentation/04/txt07_en.htm#declaration.

7 Lindley-French and Flückiger, *A Chronology of European Security and Defence 1945–2005*, 30.

8 Speech by Winston Churchill at the Council of Europe, Strasbourg, 11 August 1950. European Navigator, www.ema.lu/mce.cfm.

9 There are five other observers: Canada, Denmark, the Netherlands, Norway, and the US.

10 Lindley-French, and Flückiger, *A Chronology of European Security and Defence 1945–2005*, 43.

11 There is no specific evidence that Ismay actually said this, but this now over-used quote has been attributed to him and it has passed into NATO folklore.

12 See http://www.eurotreaties.com/eurotexts.html#rometreaty.

13 However, there were those around Kennedy, such as Albert Wohlstetter and the RAND think-tankers, who did not like the idea of independent deterrents, not just because of the loss of US control, but because they diverted resources away from improving conventional NATO forces. See Lawrence Freedman, *The Evolution of Nuclear Strategy:* Second Edition (London: Macmillan, 1989).

14 See "Declaration of the North Atlantic Council, December 16, 1958," Clause 6, www.ena.lu/mce.cfm.

15 Bruce Kuklick has written an interesting analysis of the so-called "brains trust." He points out the split between the realist/historicists of the Morgenthau and Kennan schools with the hard theorists, such as Albert Wohlstetter, Thomas Schelling, and Herman Kahn, that came out of RAND in the early 60s to advise the Kennedy administration, and not always very well, seduced by the needs of their political masters. Hedley Bull famously contrasted the "classical" and "scientific" approaches to international relations. See Bruce Kuklick, *Blind Oracles: Intellectuals and War from Kennan to Kissinger* (Princeton: Princeton University Press, 2006).

16 M. von Merkatz (rapporteur), "Press Conference by President de Gaulle (Extracts)," 14 January 1963, Western European Union Assembly, General Affairs Committee, Tenth Ordinary Session (Paris, Political Union of Europe, 1964), http://aei.pitt.edu/5777/01/003749_1.pdf.

17 Kissinger himself wrote of the shift in US policy that he helped to engineer, "The survival of mankind ultimately depended on the relationship of the two superpowers, but the peace of the world depended on whether America could distinguish between those responsibilities in which its role was merely helpful and those to which it was indispensable . . . ". From Henry Kissinger, *Diplomacy* (New York: Simon & Schuster, 1994), 707.

18 "Declaration," Meeting of the Heads of State or Government, Paris, 19–21 October 1972, First Summit Conference of the Enlarged Community (Paragraph 7), Reproduced from the Bulletin of the European Communities, No. 10, 1972, http://aei.pitt.edu/1919/02/paris_1972_communique.pdf.

### 3 Coping with the Allies

1 Julian Lindley-French and Katja Flückiger, *A Chronology of European Security and Defence 1945–2005* (Geneva: Geneva Center for Security Policy, 2005), 101.

2 Charles L. Glaser identified the essential components of effective deterrence when considering the US/Soviet nuclear stand-off in the 1960s, "Soviet leaders will be deterred if . . . the *probability* that the United States will carry out the threat combined with the *costs* if the threat is carried out is greater than the *probability* that the Soviet Union can accomplish the contemplated action with the *benefits* they can expect to derive from it." Charles L. Glaser, *Analyzing Strategic Nuclear Policy* (Princeton: Princeton University Press, 1990), 20.

3 "Communiqué," Meeting of the Heads of Government, Paris, 9–10 December 1974, http://aei.pitt.edu/1459/01/Paris_1974.pdf.

4 The Forward Base System envisaged the forward deployment of US nuclear-capable aircraft in Europe to re-assure the European Allies that strategic arms limitation talks would not lead to de-coupling. However, the Randians, in particular, believed these forces so vulnerable to Soviet attack that they lowered the nuclear threshold.

5 Raymond Garthoff writes, "Eurocommunism was the term coined in 1975–76 to denote the new current of Western European communism that stressed independence of action for each party and embodied varying degrees of democratic and pluralistic tendencies." See Raymond L. Garthoff, *Détente and Confrontation: American–Soviet Relations from Nixon to Reagan* (Washington: Brookings Institution Press, 1985), 490.

6 Lindley-French and Flückiger, *A Chronology of European Security and Defence 1945–2005*, 105.

7 Ibid., 107.

8 Ibid., 109.

9 Ibid., 112.

10 The Second Cold War is a phrase coined by Professor Fred Halliday. He looks at the Cold War as structured slightly differently to this author, "Cold War II is the most recent of four major phases into which post-1945 history can be divided . . . They are: Phase I, the First Cold War 1946–53; Phase II, the period of Oscillatory Antagonism 1953–69; Phase III, Détente, 1969–79; Phase IV, The Second Cold War, 1979 onwards." See Fred Halliday, ed., *The Making of the Second Cold War* (London: Verso Books, 1989), 3.

11 Gompert, Kugler and Libicki make the point effectively: "In the two decades are the Vietnam War, the United States invested heavily in the technologies that would enable it to project power, penetrate enemy airspace, and use strike forces to thwart a large-scale armoured offensive . . . the European allies, being preoccupied with the defense of their borders, concentrated on relatively stationary 'main defense formations'." David C. Gompert, Richard L. Kugler and Martin C. Libicki, *Mind the Gap: Promoting a Transatlantic Revolution in Military Affairs* (Washington: National Defense University Press, 1999), 13.

12 See Walter LaFeber, *America, Russia and the Cold War 1945–1990* (New York: McGraw-Hill, 1991), 302.

13 European Council, "Solemn Declaration on European Union," Stuttgart, 19 June 1983 (the Stuttgart Declaration), reproduced from the Bulletin of the European Communities, No. 6/1983, http://aei.pitt.edu/1788/01/ stuttgart_declaration_1983.pdf.

14 Declaration of the Council of Ministers of the Western European Union, Rome, 26–27 October 1984 (the Rome Declaration), http://www.weu.int/ documents/841024en.pdf.

15 Lindley-French and Flückiger, *A Chronology of European Security and Defence 1945–2005*, 130.

16 Although James Baker, the US Secretary of State, did not negotiate INF he offers some interesting insights into American thinking. "The INF Treaty was a breakthrough in that it not only eliminated an entire class of nuclear weapons, it codified two principles that would become critical to Bush [senior] arms-control policy. To get to zero weapons, the Kremlin, which had much higher levels of forces, had to make larger cuts than the West. This concept of 'asymmetrical reductions' became critical when we discussed conventional arms, in which Soviet advantages were even greater. In addition, the treaty also required extensive, intrusive verification regimes. Previously, arms control had generally relied on 'national technical means' – namely, spy satellites. The INF Treaty made on-site inspections a reality." James A. Baker III, *The Politics of Diplomacy: Revolution, War and Peace 1989–1992* (New York: Putnam, 1995), 84.

17 Western European Union, "Platform on European Security Interests," The Hague, 27 October 1987, http://www.weu.int/documents/871027en.pdf.

18 North Atlantic Council, "Final Communiqué," Brussels, 11 December 1987, http://www.nato.int/docu/comm/49–95/c871211a.htm.

## 4 Strategic Vacation

1 The North Atlantic Treaty Organization, "The Alliance's New Strategic Concept, Part IV – Guidelines for Defense, Paragraph 46" agreed by the Heads of State and Government, North Atlantic Council, Rome, 7–8 November 1991, www.nato.int/docu/comm/49–95/c911107a.htm.

2 President Reagan said: "And then John Winthrop, who would later become the first Governor of Massachusetts, reminded his fellow Puritans there on that tiny deck that they must keep faith with their God, that the eyes of all the world were upon them, and that they must not forsake the mission that God had sent them on, and they must be a light unto the nations of all the world – a shining city upon a hill." See the Archives of the Ronald Reagan Presidential Library, "Remarks at the Opening Ceremonies of the Statue of Liberty Centennial in New York, New York, 3 July 1986," http://www.reagan. utexas.edu/search/speeches/speech_srch. html.

3 In 1992 Francis Fukuyama wrote, "Assuming that liberal democracy is, for the moment, safe from external enemies, could we assume that successful democratic societies could remain that way indefinitely? Or is liberal democracy prey to serious internal contradictions, contradictions so serious that they will eventually undermine it as a political system? There is no doubt that contemporary democracies face any number of serious problems, from drugs, homelessness and crime to environmental damage

and the frivolity of consumerism." Francis Fukuyama, *The End of History and the Last Man* (London: Hamish Hamilton, 1992), xxi.

4  The North Atlantic Council, "London Declaration on a Transformed North Atlantic Alliance issued by the Heads of State and Government participating in the meeting of the North Atlantic Council," London, 5–6 July 1990, http://www.nato.int/docu/comm/49–95/c900706a.htm.

5  Whilst focused determinedly on the economic relationship and establishing bi-annual consultations between the European Community and the US, the Declaration affirms that "To achieve their common goals, the European Community, and its Member-States and the United States of America will inform and consult each other on important matters of common interest . . . " The Declaration does not mention NATO by name, merely suggesting, "In appropriate international bodies . . . they will seek close cooperation." In some respects, this is the start of a direct US–EC relationship that some have feared will one day eclipse NATO. See http://europa.eu.int/comm/external_relations/us/economic_partnership/declaration_1990.htm.

6  Treaty on European Union, Provisions of a Common Foreign and Security Policy, Title V, Article J.4.1, December 1991, http://europa.eu.int/en/record/mt/top.html.

7  Julian Lindley-French and Katja Flückiger, *A Chronology of European Security and Defence 1945–2005* (Geneva: Geneva Center for Security Policy), 159.

8  NATO, "The Alliance's New Strategic Concept, agreed by the Heads of State and Government," Rome, 7–8 November 1991, http://www.nato.int/docu/comm/49–95/c911107a.htm.

9  In his 2004 article in *Foreign Affairs*, Professor Joseph Nye coined the phrase "soft power" to distinguish it against the hard power of armed force, as part of a balanced and broad set of state tools for effective foreign engagement. See Joseph S. Nye, "The Decline of America's Soft Power," *Foreign Affairs* 83, No. 3, May/June 2004, 16–20.

10  Western European Union, "Petersberg Declaration," Section II, Paragraph 4,Western European Union, Council of Ministers, Bonn, 19 June 1992, http://www.weu.int/documents/920619peten.pdf.

11  Clinton's focus was cutting the budget deficit of the Reagan years and offering a middle-class tax cut but he was no lightweight on matters international. In his memoirs he writes of the importance of NATO as the Berlin Wall fell, "Our long stand-off against communist expansion was ending with the victory of freedom, thanks to the united front presented by NATO and the constancy of American leaders from Harry Truman to George Bush." See Bill Clinton, *My Life* (New York: Alfred A. Knopf, 2004), 353

12  Lindley-French and Flückiger, *A Chronology of European Security and Defence 1945–2005*, 175.

13  NATO, "Final Communiqué," Paragraph 4, Defense Planning Committee and Nuclear Planning Group (NATO Press Communiqué M-DPC/NPG-2(93)75), Brussels, 9 December 1993, http://www.nato.int/docu/comm/49–95/c931209a.htm.

14  NATO, "Declaration of the Heads of State and Government," Ministerial Meeting of the North Atlantic Council/North Atlantic Cooperation

Council, Brussels, 11 January 1994, http://www.nato.int/docu/comm/49–95/c940111a.htm.

15 Lindley-French and Flückiger, *A Chronology of European Security and Defence 1945–2005*, 182.

## 5 The Search for a New Strategic Consensus

1 Maartje Rutten, ed., "From St Malo to Nice – European Defense: Core Documents," *Chaillot Papers* 47 (Paris: Western European Union – Institute for Security Studies, 2001), 11.

2 To be fair, Madeleine Albright is illuminating on Clinton's view of NATO. "By the time President Clinton took office, an obvious question had arisen. With no superpower enemy, why NATO? The President's answer was that it remained the cornerstone of European security. Although the Soviet threat had vanished, other threats such as terrorism, the proliferation of weapons of mass destruction, and ethnic cleansing had taken its place." Madeleine K. Albright, *Madam Secretary: A Memoir* (London: Macmillan, 2003), 253.

3 These suspicions were to come to a head in 1997. As Human Rights Watch puts it, "The US distrust was mainly based on an incident from mid-1997, when the US discovered that a French liaison officer in Bosnia, Herve Gourmelon, was leaking plans of [Radovan] Karadzic's arrest . . . The French Defense Ministry claimed that the liaison officer had 'maintained various contacts consonant with his orders' and denied these contacts jeopardized the arrest." See www.hrw.org/backgrounder/cea/srebrenica.

4 Differently to the 1990 Declaration this one affirms the role of NATO, as it states, "We affirm the indivisibility of transatlantic security, NATO remains, for its member, the center-piece of transatlantic security, providing the indispensable link between North America and Europe." The European Union and The United States of America, "The New Transatlantic Agenda," Madrid, December 1995, http://europa.eu.int/comm/external_relations/us/new_transatlantic_agenda/text.htm.

5 NATO, "Founding Act on Mutual Relations, Cooperation and Security between NATO and the Russian Federation," Paris, 27 May 1997, www.nato.int/docu/basictxt/fndact-a.htm.

6 Rutten, "From St Malo to Nice – European Defense: Core Documents," 3.

7 The St Malo Declaration, 3–4 December 1998. See Rutten, "From St Malo to Nice – European Defense: Core Documents," 8.

8 See Madeleine K. Albright, "The Right Balance will Secure NATO's Future," *Financial Times*, 7 December 1998. See Rutten, "From St Malo to Nice – European Defense: Core Documents," 10–11.

9 General Wesley Clark, SACEUR at the time of Kosovo, puts it this way, "As for NATO, political approval from each member nation has been necessary before any military plans can be developed, the general political reluctance in the West to signal readiness to use force means that the Alliance's military planning will almost inevitably be too slow. When called to act, the plans are unlikely to go far enough to deal with the range of contingencies that might arise." See Wesley K. Clark, *Waging Modern War: Bosnia, Kosovo and the Future of Combat* (New York: Public Affairs Press, 2001), 422.

10  *NATO Handbook* (Brussels: North Atlantic Treaty Organization, 2001), 44.
11  *NATO Handbook*, 44.
12  *NATO Handbook*, 46.
13  George H.W. Bush, "Remarks by the President in Address to Faculty and Students of Warsaw University," Warsaw, Poland, 15 June 2001, www.whitehouse.gov/news/releases/2001/06/20010615-1.html.

## 6  NATO Today

1  *NATO Handbook* (Brussels: North Atlantic Treaty Organization, 2001), 527.
2  All above figures from the *NATO Handbook*.
3  IISS *Military Balance 2005–2006* identifies them as 17 E-3A Sentry aircraft. See Christopher Langton, ed., *The Military Balance 2005–2006* (London: Routledge, 2005), 81.
4  European Council, "Presidency Conclusions," European Defense: NATO/ EU Consultations, Planning and Operations, 17 and 18 June 2004, http://ue.eu.int/uedocs/cmsUpload/81742.pdf.
5  Throughout the Cold War, interoperability was a problem for the Alliance. As Rob de Wijk writes, "Interoperability was considered to be a problem because all allies used different 'how-to-fight' manuals. In contrast to the Warsaw Pact, no single NATO doctrine existed and there was even no formal NATO guidance for the development of national doctrines. To harmonize the doctrinal efforts, NATO developed Allied Publications (AP) providing the national authorities with information pertaining to tactics, intelligence, doctrine, security rules, exercise procedures, and technical and administrative matters. These documents provided a basis for the improvement of interoperability." Rob de Wijk, *The Art of Military Coercion: Why the West's Military Superiority Scarcely Matters* (Amsterdam: Mets & Schild, 2004), 135.
6  There is a lot of debate about just what doctrine actually is. Basically it is how militaries do things and the communication thereof to all concerned. However, it can get very pompous. Rob de Wijk says, "Doctrine defines the nature and characteristics of current and future military operations, preparation for those operations in peacetime, and the methods for successfully completing military operations in times of conflict." De Wijk, *The Art of Military Coercion: Why the West's Military Superiority Scarcely Matters*, 126.
7  See "Capabilities Improvement Chart II/2005," Brussels, 21 November 2005, http://ue.eu.int/ueDocs/newsWord/en/misc/87106.doc.
8  Hans Binnendijk, David C. Gompert and Richard L. Kugler, "A New Military Framework for NATO," *Defense Horizons*, no. 48 (May 2005), 8.
9  Author's own research elaborated in Julian Lindley-French and Franco Algieri, *A European Defence Strategy* (Gütesloh: Bertelsmann Stiftung, 2004).
10  Lindley-French and Algieri, *A European Defence Strategy*.
11  Lindley-French and Algieri, *A European Defence Strategy*.
12  See Michèle A. Flournoy and Julianne Smith, eds, *European Defense Integration: Bridging the Gap Between Strategy and Capabilities* (Washington: Center for Strategic and International Studies, 2005), 31.

13 Senator Richard Lugar coined that phrase in the early 90s to mean that NATO had to take responsibility for Europe as a whole. However, in a speech to the Council on Foreign Relations, on 4 March 2002, he said, "In a world in which terrorist 'Article 5' attacks on our countries can be planned in Germany, financed in Asia and carried out in the US, old distinctions between 'in' and 'out' of area have become meaningless." Richard G. Lugar, "NATO After 9/11: Crisis or Opportunity?", Council on Foreign Relations, 4 March 2002, http://www.cfr.org/ publication.html?id = 4379.

14 The British know how to do these operations but their numbers are extremely limited. Dana Priest, in her book *The Mission*, relates a revealing conversation in Afghanistan that extends to all Europeans. "The British had agreed to lead the ISAF operation. Now they wanted out. The Turks, who had promised to take over from the British, were slow on the uptake, and they would soon abandon the job. For post-war Kosovo, nine-teen NATO nations and a dozen non-NATO ones had sent peacekeepers and police officers. The police in Kosovo weren't very effective, but at least they showed up. In Afghanistan, they weren't even showing up. 'There's real concern in Europe that we don't walk out of here and leave the place,' said squadron leader Tom Rounds of the Royal Air Force, describing Britain's attitude as he sat on a pile of wooden boxes at Bagram base. As for positioning peacekeepers throughout the country, he moaned, 'We just don't have the troops to do that. It would take thousands. Where are you going to get them?'" Dana Priest, *The Mission: Waging War and Keeping Peace with America's Military* (New York: Norton, 2003), 389.

15 Lindley-French and Algieri, *A European Defence Strategy*.

16 Lindley-French and Algieri, *A European Defence Strategy*.

## 7 The Past, Present and Future of NATO

1 *The National Security Strategy of the United States of America* (Washington: The Office of the President of the United States, 2006), 38.

2 IISS writes, "The modernisation and reform of China's armed forces, challenging the US and its allies, is one of the main defense issues in east and northeast Asia. Washington has had concerns about the growth in Chinese military power for some time. The US Department of Defense Report, 'The Military Power of the People's Republic of China,' released 19 July 2005, demonstrated Washington's concern at what it sees as a Chinese military build-up, not only directed towards Taiwan, but also aimed at developing force projection capabilities beyond Chinese waters." Christopher Langton, ed., *The Military Balance 2005–2006* (London: Routledge, 2005), 259.

3 Thomas Barnett puts it this way: "Despite being the world's sole military superpower, America needs to understand that it stands on the cusp of a new multipolar era defined by globalization's progressive advance. It also needs to realize that emerging global conflict lies between those who want to see the world grow ever more connected and rule-bound and those who want to isolate large chunks of humanity from the globalization process . . . ". The same goes for Europeans, if not more so. Thomas P. M.

Barnett, *The Pentagon's New Map: War and Peace in the Twenty-First Century* (New York: Putnam, 2004), 32.

4 General Sir Rupert Smith makes the point clearly, " . . . for force to be effective the desired outcome of its use must be understood in such detail that the context of its uses is defined as well as the application. The general purpose of all interventions is clear: we seek to establish in the minds of the people and their leaders that the ever-present option of conflict is not the preferable course of action when in confrontation over some matter or other." General Sir Rupert Smith, *The Utility of Force: The Art of War in the Modern World* (London: Allen Lane, 2005), 398.

5 Jolyon Howorth has given the most compelling definition of ESDP that most leaders would subscribe to. ESDP is a "project to confer upon the EU the ability to take collective decisions relating to regional security and to deploy a range of instruments, including military instruments, in operations of crisis management, peacekeeping, and, if necessary, peace enforcement (preferably with a legal mandate), as a distinctive European contribution to the overall objectives of the Atlantic Alliance and in consultation with both European members of NATO and non-allies EU accession candidates." See Jolyon Howorth, "Why ESDP is Necessary and Beneficial for the Alliance," *Defending Europe: The EU, NATO and the Quest for European Autonomy*, ed. Jolyon Howorth and John T. S. Keeler (New York: Palgrave Macmillan, 2003), 221.

6 The Thirty Years War took place between 1618 and 1648, principally on the territory of today's Germany. Noted for its savagery, the main contention was a struggle for ascendancy between fundamentalist Catholic and Protestant beliefs.

7 Effect is the achievement of one's objectives and that means power, i.e. the resources, organization and application through various means. Max Weber's definition of power is as good as any. Power is the possibility of imposing one's will upon the behavior of other persons. From John K. Galbraith, "Power and Organization," in *Power*, ed. Steven Lukes (Oxford: Blackwells, 1986), 212.

# Bibliography and Further Reading

## Strategy

Barnett, Thomas, P. M., *The Pentagon's New Map: War and Peace in the Twenty-First Century* (New York: Putnam, 2004). One Pentagon insider looks at the relationship between globalization and security governance.

Bergen, Peter L., *Holy War Inc – Inside the Secret World of Osama Bin Laden* (London: Weidenfeld Nicolson, 2001). An insight into the thinking, nature and structure of strategic terrorism.

Bobbit, Philip, *The Shield of Achilles – War, Peace and the Course of History* (London: Penguin, 2003). Bobbit considers a broad sweep of history to demonstrate the power of the global market in shaping the very nature of the state.

Codevilla, Angelo M., *No Victory, No Peace* (Lanham: Rowman & Littlefield, 2005). An analysis of the complexities of modern security, making security policy and declaring victory.

European Union, *A Secure Europe in a Better World: The European Security Strategy* (Paris: European Union – Institute for Security Studies, 2004). The EU's December 2003 European Security Strategy.

Garton-Ash, Timothy, *Free World – Why a Crisis of the West Reveals the Opportunity of Our Time* (London: Allen Lane, 2004). A call for the West to be re-generated in pursuit of its idealist and realist goals.

Huldt, Bo, et al., *Strategic Yearbook 2006* (Stockholm: Swedish National Defense College, 2006). The 2006 annual analysis of the changing strategic environment.

Kaplan, Robert D., *Warrior Politics – Why Leadership Demands a Pagan Ethos* (New York: Random House, 2002). An application of classical security theory to the modern world.

Kissinger, Henry, *Does America Need a Foreign Policy? Towards a Diplomacy for the Twenty-First Century* (New York: Touchstone, 2001). An analysis of the impact of power upon classical foreign policy.

Kupchan, Charles A., *The End of the American Era* (New York: Alfred A. Knopf, 2002). What to do with American foreign and security policy as Pax Americana gives way to strategic uncertainty.

Lake, Anthony, *Six Nightmares* (Boston: Little, Brown and Co., 2002). Six scenarios for asymmetric attack, from a former National Security Advisor.

Lindley-French, Julian, *Terms of Engagement: The Paradox of American Power and the Transatlantic Dilemma Post-11 September* (Paris: European Union –

Institute for Security Studies, 2002). An analysis of the dilemma of classical great power in a non-classical world.

——, "Euronukes?" *Aspenia*, nos.27–28, 2005 (Rome: Aspen). An analysis of the non-role of British and French nuclear weapons in European defense.

——, "The Revolution in Security Affairs: Hard and Soft Security Dynamics in the Twenty-First Century," in Anne Aldis and Graeme P. Herd (eds) *Soft Security Threats and European Security* (London: Routledge, 2005). An analysis of the gaps within Europe over the use of coercion.

Lindley-French, Julian and Franco Algieri, *Why Europe Needs to Be Strong . . . and the World Needs a Strong Europe* (Gütesloh, Bertelsmann Stiftung, 2005). A plea to the 2005 December European Council to take European defense seriously.

Lukes, Steven, ed., *Power* (Oxford: Blackwells, 1986). Series of essays by the great and the good on the nature and definitions of power.

Mearsheimer, John J., *The Tragedy of Great Power Politics* (New York and London: Norton, 2001). A realist look at the history of power politics and why Great Powers are doomed to compete.

Smith, General Sir Rupert, *The Utility of Force: The Art of War in the Modern World* (London: Allen Lane, 2005). A study by a former senior British commander to demonstrate the possibilities and the limits of the use of force in complex political environments.

Tardy, Thierry, ed., *Peace Operations After 11 September, 2001* (London and New York: Frank Cass, 2005). A collection of essays looking at the changing context, particularly of UN peace operations in the wake of 9/11.

*The National Security Strategy of the United States of America* (Washington: The Office of the President of the United States, 2006).

De Wijk, Rob, *The Art of Military Coercion: Why the West's Military Superiority Scarcely Matters* (Amsterdam: Mers & Schildt, 2004). A look at the use of coercion and the role of armed forces in asymmetric environments.

Zaborowski, Martin, ed., *Friends Again? EU–U.S. Relations After the Crisis* (Paris: European Union – Institute for Security Studies, 2006). A series of essays looking at the state of contemporary US–EU relations.

## NATO

Allin, Dana H., "NATO's Balkan Intervention," *IISS Adelphi Paper* 377 (Oxford: Oxford University Press, 2002). An analysis of the strengths and weaknesses of NATO's engagement in the Balkans.

Binnendijk, Hans, David C. Gompert and Richard L. Kugler, "A New Military Framework for NATO," *Defense Horizons*, no. 48, May 2005 (Washington: National Defense University). Call for the further transformation of NATO to prepare it for the challenges of the twenty-first century.

Biscop, Sven, ed., *E Pluribus Unum? Military Integration in the European Union* (Brussels: Royal Institute for International Relations (IRRI-KIIB), 2005). A look at how Europeans are to close the gap between the security environment, their military capabilities and political aspirations.

Brimmer, Esther, ed., *The EU's Search for a Strategic Role* (Washington: Center for Transatlantic Relations/Johns Hopkins University, 2002). An in-depth study of the relationship between EU political cohesion and grand strategy.

David, Charles-Philippe and Jacques Levesque, eds, *The Future of NATO: Enlargement: Russia and European Security* (Montreal and Kingston:

McGill and Queens University Press, 2005). Canadian study on the future of NATO that combines theoretical, policy and analytical approaches.

Hamilton, Daniel S., *Transatlantic Transformations: Equipping NATO for the 21st Century* (Washington: Center for Transatlantic Relations/Johns Hopkins Universty, 2004). A collection of essays exploring how US military transformation can be made relevant for NATO.

Hopkinson, W., "Enlargement: A New NATO," in *Chaillot Papers* 49 (Paris: Western European Union – Institute for Security Studies, 2001). An analysis of the opportunities and challenges posed by NATO enlargement.

Howorth, Jolyon and John T. S. Keeler, *Defending Europe: The EU, NATO and the Quest for European Autonomy* (New York: Palgrave Macmillan, 2003). A collection of essays exploring the search for Europe's new security identity both within the Alliance and without.

Kaplan, Lawrence S., *The Long Entanglement: NATO's First Fifty Years* (Westport: Praeger, 1999). Detailed analysis of NATO's history from an American perspective.

Kay, Sean, *NATO and the Future of European Security* (Lanham: Rowman & Littlefield, 1998). A look at the changing nature of European security and its impact upon the Alliance.

Lindley-French, Julian, "My End is Going Down . . . Iraq and the Transatlantic Political-Security Mess," *American Foreign Policy Interests* 25: 6 (New York: National Committee on American Foreign Policy, 2003). How to save transatlantic relations from the Iraq imbroglio.

Lindley-French, Julian and Franco Algieri, *Enhancing the European Union as An International Security Actor* (Gütesloh: Bertelsmann Stiftung, 2000). How to turn European defense rhetoric into reality.

—— *A European Defence Strategy* (Gütesloh: Bertelsmann Stiftung, 2004). A further plan to turn European defense rhetoric into reality.

Moens, Alexander, Cohen Lenard, J. and Sens Allen, G., *NATO and European Security* (Westport: Praeger, 2003). Series of essays on NATO"s current and future challenges.

*The NATO Handbook* (Brussels: North Atlantic Treaty Organization, 2001). NATO's official handbook.

Papocosma, Victor S., Sean Kay, Mark R. Rubin, eds, *NATO After Fifty Years* (Wilmington, Delaware: Scholarly Resources, 2001). A series of essays providing a snapshot of NATO fifty years after its founding.

Schmidt, Gustav, ed., *A History of NATO: The First Fifty Years* (London: Praeger, 2001). A collection of essays exploring various aspects of NATO history.

Serfaty, Simon, ed., *The United States, the European Union and NATO – After the Cold War and Beyond Iraq* (Washington: Center for Strategic and International Studies, 2005). A series of essays looking at key actors in the European security architecture and how to move beyond Iraq.

**History**

Albright, Madeleine, *Madam Secretary: A Memoir* (London: Macmillan, 2003). A personal account of Mrs Albright's life and time in office.

Ambrose, Stephen E., *Rise to Globalism – American Foreign Policy Since 1938* (New York: Penguin, 1988). An analysis of the emergence of the US as a global power and how it has changed America and the world.

Baker, James A. III, *The Politics of Diplomacy: Revolution, War and Peace 1989–1992* (New York: Putnam, 1995). A detailed analysis of negotiations during a pivotal period by a former Secretary of State.

Clark, Wesley K., *Waging Modern War: Bosnia, Kosovo and the Future of Combat* (New York: Public Affairs Press, 2001). A personal account by the former Supreme Allied Commander, Europe, with a particular focus on the conduct of the Kosovo War.

Clinton, Bill, *My Life* (New York: Alfred A. Knopf, 2004). Personal account of the former president's time in office.

Freedman, Lawrence, *The Evolution of Nuclear Strategy*, Second Edition (London: Macmillan, 1989). A broad-sweep analysis of the evolution of nuclear strategy from the birth of the bomb to the end of the Cold War and into the Reagan years.

—— "The Revolution in Strategic Affairs," *IISS Adelphi Paper* 318, (Oxford: Oxford University Press, 1998). Essay exploring the need for conceptual strategic thinking in a new strategic environment.

Fukuyama, Francis, *The End of History and the Last Man* (London: Hamish Hamilton, 1992). A call for the US to make the most of its victory in the Cold War by championing liberal democracy, freedom of expression, movement and open markets.

Garthoff, Raymond L., *Détente and Confrontation: American–Soviet Relations from Nixon to Reagan* (Washington: Brookings Institution Press, 1985).

Glaser, Charles L., *Analyzing Strategic Nuclear Policy* (Princeton: Princeton University Press, 1990). An intensely detailed analysis of the politics of the Cold War from the Nixon administration to the Reagan administration.

Gnesotto, Nicole., ed., *European Security and Defence Policy – The First Five Years (1999–2004)* (Paris: European Union – Institute for Security Studies, 2004). A collection of essays exploring the performance of the ESDP.

Grosser, Alfred, ed., *The Western Alliance: European–American Relations since 1945* (London: Macmillan, 1980). A broad history of the Western Alliance from 1945 to the 1970s from a European's viewpoint.

Halliday, Fred, ed., *The Making of the Second Cold War* (London: Verso, 1989). How détente became Cold War.

Ikenberry, John G., *After Victory* (Princeton and Oxford: Princeton University Press, 2001). Historical analysis of what states do with victory, applied to the US in the wake of the Cold War.

Kampfner, John, *Blair's Wars* (London: Simon & Schuster, 2003). A journalist's view of Tony Blair and his activist security policy.

Kissinger, Henry, *Diplomacy* (New York: Simon & Schuster, 1994). The history of Realpolitik from sixteenth-century Europe to the end of the Cold War.

Kuklick, Bruce, *Blind Oracles: Intellectuals and War from Kennan to Kissinger* (Princeton: Princeton University Press, 2006). An analysis of the role of academics in strategy and policy, and their struggles with each other and those in power.

LaFeber, Walter, *America, Russia and the Cold War 1945–1990*, 6th Edition (New York: McGraw-Hill, 1991). Historical overview of the Cold War.

Lindley-French, Julian, "In the Shade of Locarno: Why European Defense is Failing," *International Affairs* 78: 4 (2002). Historical study of why democratic European security and defense policy has always been slow to react to change.

Meyer, C., *DC Confidential* (London: Weidenfeld & Nicolson, 2005). Personal recollections of a former British ambassador to Washington.

Priest, Dana, *The Mission: Waging War and Keeping Peace with America's Military* (New York: Norton, 2003). The personal view of an American journalist embedded with American forces peacekeeping in dangerous places.

## Military/Technical

Adams, Gordon, Guy Ben-Ari, John Logsdon and Ray Williamson, *Bridging the Gap: European C4ISR and Transatlantic Interoperability* (Washington: The George Washington University, 2004). A detailed look at the gap between the capabilities of US and European forces.

Center for Research and Education on Strategy and Technology (CREST), *Coalition Military Operations: The Way Ahead Through Co-operability – Report of a French–German–UK–US Working Group* (Arlington, Virginia: US Center for Research and Education on Strategy and Technology, 2000). Analysis by a "steering committee" of the conduct of future military coalitions.

Center for Research and Education on Strategy and Technology (CREST), *Future Military Coalitions: The Transatlantic Challenge, Report of a French–German–UK–US Working Group* (Arlington, Virginia: US Center for Research and Education on Strategy and Technology, 2002). Further elaboration by a "steering committee" of the challenges posed by future military coalitions.

Flournoy, Michèle A., ed., *QDR 2001: Strategy Driven Choices for America's Security* (Washington: National Defense University, 2001). One insider's look at the policy and planning drivers behind the 2001 Quadrennial Review.

Flournoy, Michèle A., and Julianne Smith, eds., *European Defense Integration: Bridging the Gap Between Strategy and Capabilities* (Washington: Center for Strategic and International Studies, 2005). In-depth CSIS study of the challenges facing European defense integration and its relationship to the US and NATO.

Gompert, David C., Richard L. Kugler and Martin C. Libicki, *Mind the Gap: Promoting a Transatlantic Revolution in Military Affairs* (Washington: National Defense University, 1999). A warning of the military-technical gap within the Alliance, and proposals for how to close it.

Hagman, Hans-Christian, "European Crisis Management and Defense: The Search for Capabilities," *IISS Adelphi Papers* 353 (Oxford: Oxford University Press, 2002). A European study into the capabilities gap between European defense and its missions.

Heisbourg, François, ed., "European Defense: Making it Work," *Chaillot Papers* 42 (Paris: Western European Union – Institute for Security Studies, 2000). High-level study of how to move forwards in European defense.

Langton, Christopher, ed., *The Military Balance 2005–2006* (London: Routledge, 2005). Annual analysis of defense commitments and armed forces of the world's states.

Lutz, Rachel Anne, *Military Capabilities for a European Defence* (Copenhagen: Danish Institute of International Affairs, 2001). An analysis of European military deficiencies and how to resolve them.

Sarotte, Mary-Elise, "German Military Reform and European Security," *IISS Adelphi Paper* 340 (Oxford: Oxford University Press, 2001). An analysis of the political, economic and military difficulties associated with reforming the German armed forces.

Thomas, James P., "The Military Challenges of Transatlantic Coalitions," *IISS Adelphi Paper* 333 (Oxford: Oxford University Press, 2000). The problems of coalitions involving forces with very different capabilities, traditions and political rule of engagement.

**Reference**

Haines, Jean-Yves. ed., "From Laeken to Copenhagen, European Defense: Core Documents 2003," vol. III. *Chaillot Papers* 57 (Paris: European Union – Institute for Security Studies, 2003). Collection of official documents.

Korteweg, Rem, *The Discourse on European Defence* (The Hague: Clingendael, 2005). A collection of core documents and speeches relevant to European security and defense.

Lindley-French, Julian and Katja Flückiger, *A Chronology of European Security and Defence 1945–2005* (Geneva: Geneva Center for Security Policy, 2005). Blow by blow timeline of European security and defense.

Rutten, Maartje, ed., "From St Malo to Nice – European Defense: Core Documents," *Chaillot Papers* 47 (Paris: Western European Union – Institute for Security Studies, 2001). Collection of official documents.

—— "From Nice to Laeken, European Defense: Core Documents," vol. II, *Chaillot Paper* 51 (Paris: European Union – Institute for Security Studies, 2002). Collection of official documents.

**Online Sources**

| | |
|---|---|
| Charles de Gaulle Archive | www.charlesdegaulle.org |
| CNN | www.cnnstudentnews.com |
| Council on Foreign Relations | www.cfr.org |
| European Union Council of Ministers | http://ue.eu.int |
| European Union online at: | http://europa.eu.int |
| Eurotreaties at: | www.eurotreaties.com |
| European Navigator at: | www.ena.lu/mce.cfm |
| European Defense at: | www.european-defence.com |
| Keesings On-line Archive | www.keesing.com |
| The Heritage Foundation | www.heritage.org |
| Human Rights Watch | www.hrw.org |
| NATO | www.nato.int |
| Source Watch | www.sourcewatch.org |
| Western European Union | www.weu.int |
| World-wide School | www.worldwideschool.org |
| Yale University | www.yale.edu |

# Index